SHOULD WE READ <u>ONLY</u> THE KING JAMES BIBLE

Are Modern Translations Evil?

DAN & SONYA CARLSON

© Copyright 2019 Dan & Sonya Carlson

Dedicated to the King of Kings

"They read from the Book of the Law of God,
making it clear and giving the meaning
so that people could understand what was being read"
(Nehemiah 8:8 NIV).

This book was first published in 2006 under the title "*Very Naughty Figs*" by Trafford Publishing.

Authors Dan and Sonya Carlson live on a small ranch in Salome, Arizona, and pastor the Bible Church in Aguila.

Dan spent his youth in Ecuador, South America, as a missionary's kid, and is a 1950 graduate of Missionary Training Institute in Nyack, NY. Other books he's written include: *Prophetic Visions Warn America*, *The Ins and Outs of Mormonism*, and *Uprooting the Mountain of Death*.

Sonya is a delightful cartoonist, and her drawings in this book say it all! She raises a small heard of Nubian goats (and is known locally as "The Goat Lady") The drawings were inspired by some of the quaint and archaic sayings in the KJV Bible. They're created to give you a chuckle or two. Happy Smiles!

ISBN: 978-1-7332105-1-5

Dan & Sonya Carlson
PO Box 726 Salome, Arizona 85348

Table of Contents

INTRODUCTION 1

CHAPTER ONE 3
    THE KING JAMES BIBLE LEGACY

CHAPTER TWO 15
    SCRIBAL & TRANSLATOR ERRORS

CHAPTER THREE 55
    CHRIST'S DIVINE NATURE

CHAPTER FOUR 83
    SELECTED ARCHAISMS

INTRODUCTION

We praise God He's given us the ability to appreciate humor — and also for our response to it — laughter. In Psalm 2, we read that God Himself looked down and laughed — and the context shows He's laughing at the man who is taking himself too seriously.

Nothing is more sacred to us than the precious Word of God. But language has changed in the last 400 years. Many words and expressions have new meanings — some of them comical.

God wants us to know Him, to understand Him as much as we are able. To stubbornly demand usage of a word that is no longer understood, to insist that our translation has a corner on truth is, very simply, pride.

And isn't that what God was laughing at?

CHAPTER ONE

The King James Bible Legacy

I (Dan) grew up on the King James Version. Most of the Bible verses I've memorized over the years are from that beloved classic.

It's been a close companion for as far back as I can remember — the source of much inspiration and encouragement.

This dear old friend still keeps beckoning me to share quiet moments together.

For hundreds of years, English-speaking Christians have relied on the King James for their comfort and peace.

Millions have lived and even died for it.

Its memorialized sayings are inscribed on stately government buildings. The Ten Commandments are engraved on courthouse walls. In America's early years, our founding fathers sprinkled their documents and formal speeches with King James sayings.

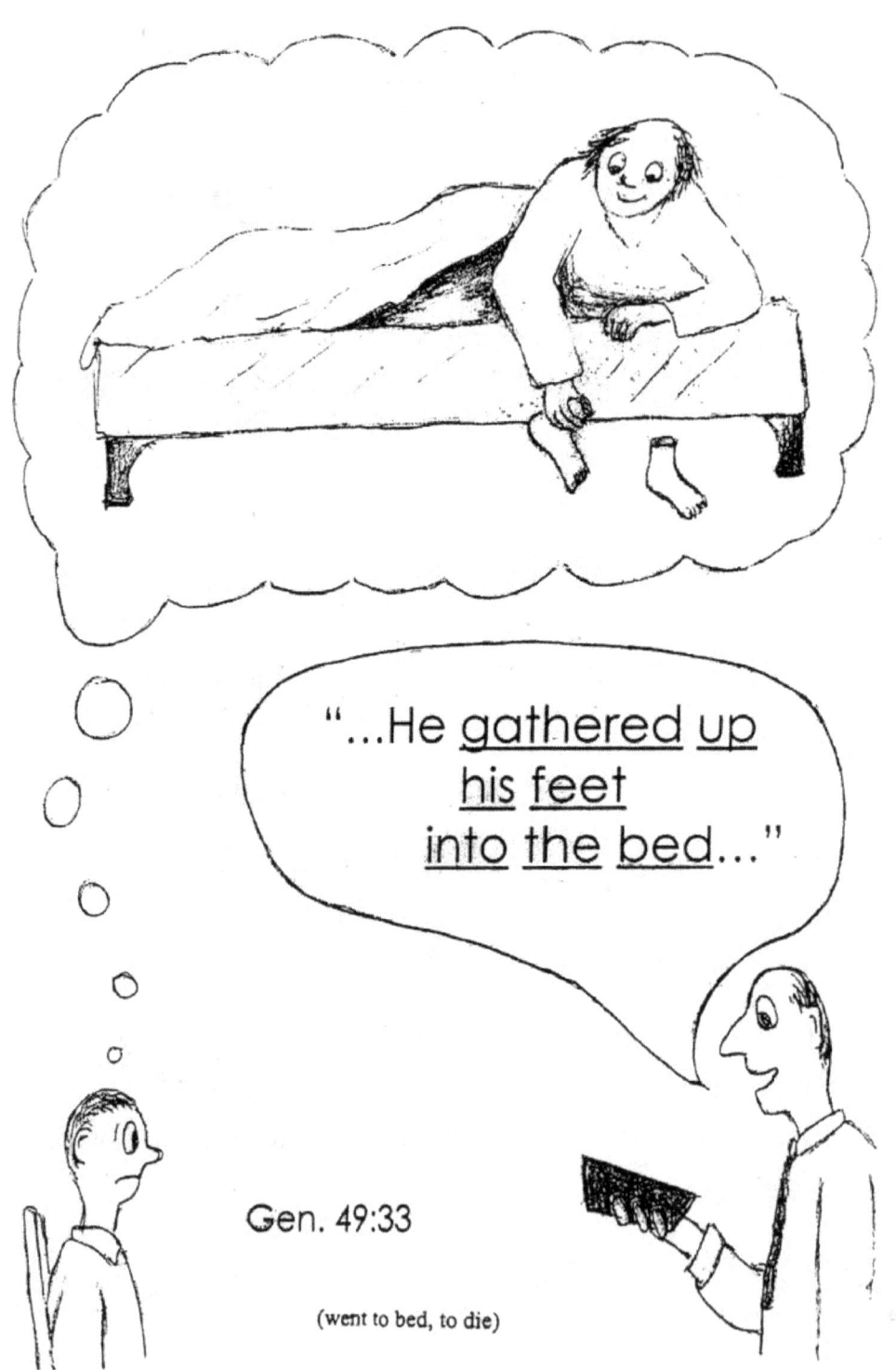

It was the official textbook in elementary schools and required reading in many high schools and colleges. America grew up with the King James Version and our generation owes it a debt of gratitude.

It is recognized by many as having unsurpassed literary quality and its poetic beauty is widely acclaimed.

For those of us belonging to the *over-the-hill-bunch*, its prose and style stir in us nostalgic emotions and fond memories of spiritual feasts.

Many of our attitudes and actions have been shaped by its lofty ideals and cloaked in its familiar proverbs and truisms.

KJV Limitations

Having said all that, the fact remains that the King James Version has a few disadvantages.

For one, its quaint style and frequent **archaisms** make it less understandable than it was four hundred years ago when *King James English* was the language of the day.

That's an undeniable fact! Let's face it; languages have a way of evolving. As cultures and societies change, so do words and definitions. New words and and new meanings to old words are created to accommodate current demands.

That's what the drawings in this book illustrate. My wife, co-author Sonya Carlson, has a talent for picturing a child's thoughts as he hears some of these curious, archaic expressions.

That's not to say our contemporary style of speech is superior. It's merely being aware of the fact that 21st century English is not the same as that spoken in 1611.

Recognizing this problem has prompted devout men in our day to make the Bible more understandable to our generation. There are biblical scholars who have devoted their entire lives to the study and discipline necessary to translate the sacred words of a holy God into today's language.

Their heartfelt prayer has been that it may be better understood by those who need it the most — which includes all of us.

(For a sampling of archaic words and expressions found in the King James Bible see **Chapter Four**.)

Why the King James Version Was Published

I have a 1611 Edition of the King James Version in my library. In its "*Introduction*" it gives the reason for its creation (which happens to be the same reason for the existence of modern versions today) — that God's Word may be better understood by the common folk!

"The language of the *Wyclifite* versions [English versions then in existence] was fast becoming *obsolete*...

"William Tyndale [who published the New Testament into English from the original Greek in 1536] was determined that there should be an English Bible which not merely merchants but **ploughboys** [common laborers] could buy and read" (p. 6).

"How shall men meditate in that which they cannot understand? How shall they understand that which is kept close[d] in an unknown tongue?" (A message from *The Translators to the Readers*, p. 3, emphasis added).

Did you get that?

The King James Version was also printed so that the common ploughboys could understand it! After all, it had been some 80 years since the English Tyndale version had been published, and they wanted something more up-to-date!

Do you know how long it's been since the King James Version was published? Over 400 years!

According to the Bible, God takes a special interest in assuring us that His Word is as clear and understandable as possible (see Nehemiah 8:8).

Archaeological Finds Provide Greater Accuracy

The second problem with the King James Version is that since the time it was published, older and more reliable manuscripts, containing significant portions of various books of the Bible, have been unearthed. Thank God for allowing archaeologists to find such great treasures!

The discovery of the Dead Sea Scrolls at Qumran in 1947, plus many other astounding discoveries of biblical manuscripts, have given us a wealth of ancient portions of Scripture, some of them pre-dating existing copies by as much as a thousand years. *That's nothing to sneeze at!*

It's a fact that the closer one gets time-wise to the original writings, the more accurate they tend to be. That's because the probability of **scribal oversights** and **translator's errors** is reduced.

The Game of Gossip

It's like the parlor game of *Gossip*, where the first person whispers a secret to the second in line, who in turn passes it on to the next, until the secret gets all the way down the line. The last person then speaks out the message as he hears it.

It's amazing how different the final version is from the original. Sometimes you can't even recognize it.

Again, the closer we get to the original writings, the more accurate they tend to be.

(For examples of *scribal copying errors* and *translator oversights*, from the King James Bible itself, see **Chapter Two**.)

CHAPTER TWO

Scribal & Translator Errors

Do Bible-believing Christians accept that God gave us His inspired Word free from errors in the original manuscripts? *Of course we do!* (At least most of us do.)

We also believe that even throughout centuries of copying and recopying these ancient translations, He's kept it relatively free from serious doctrinal errors.

He did, however, permit a few scribal copying errors to survive. Perhaps that's because God, in His sovereignty (and knowing the all-too-human tendencies of His children), wanted to keep us from **worshiping** material objects — even something as sacred as His Written Word!

The fact is that not a single page of a single manuscript of the original inspired writings has ever been unearthed.

If any original scroll had managed to survive almost two thousand years of history, I suspect it would have been

venerated to the point of idol worship. And God is not about to share His glory with another person — or another *object*.

We believe that perfect inspiration is found only in the error-free manuscripts of the original, inspired writings.

In copying and recopying these sacred scrolls, even hundreds of times, it's inevitable that errors would have crept in. After all, scribes and translators were human beings, and all humans are prone to error.

Scribal Errors at a Minimum

Fortunately for us, and considering the amount of time that's elapsed, the frequency of scribal oversights and mistranslations is minimal. Serious doctrinal questions have generally not arisen due to these errors. That's the great news!

Without question, the Lord wants us to have His message in the most accurate, understandable wording possible (see Nehemiah 8:8).

For the most part, scribes and translators were dedicated, conscientious and capable men who took great pains in the transcription of manuscripts.

Is the KJV the _Only_ Authentic Version Today?

Some people are understandably troubled by the appearance of so many Bible versions on the book shelves today.

They feel that the KJV is tried and true, and has stood the test of time.

(It still out-sells any of the other versions.) And year-in-year-out it's one of the best sellers of all books — secular or religious.

Bill Graham Evangelistic Assn. Promotes The Living Bible!

Shortly after Ken Taylor completed his paraphrased translation of the Living New Testament, I understand that Billy Graham was so impressed with the liveliness and clarity of the message, that he had hundreds of thousands of copies distributed to those making decisions for Christ in his crusades.

Young and old alike have been blessed to read the Word of God in a language they could understand. Countless thousands sent in _Decision Cards_, confessing their commitment to accept Jesus Christ as Lord and Savior.

Unfounded Claims Regarding The King James Version

Unfortunately, there are a significant number of believers who have been sold on the idea that there are absolutely **no** errors in the KJV Bible. They say *no errors whatsoever*! No scribal oversights, no translator's mistakes, no errors — **period**!

Promoters of what has come to be known as the *King James Version Only* (KJV Only) movement are making claims that just don't hold up — claims that completely fly in the face of the *facts*! And we'll prove it in just a moment from the King James Bible itself!

Is it really honoring to the KJV to make false claims about it?

If anything, it creates suspicion and confusion. Believe me; the King James Version can hold its own. It's respected enough to stand on *truth* and *authenticity*. It doesn't need anyone bolstering it up with exaggerated or unfounded claims.

The KJV Only Position in a Nutshell

What do the *KJV Only* advocates really claim about the 1611 version of the Bible? One of their promoters concludes in his book, *Let's Weigh the Evidence* (by Berry Burton), with this claim: "We do have God's Holy Word today! It is *perfect* and *without error!* (p. 94, emphasis added).

Other assertions he makes are: "There can only be **one absolutely true**, inerrant (without error), infallible (without failing), Word of God" (p. 74, emphasis in original).

Guess which version he's talking about.

Zeroing in on preachers, author Burton declares: "If you don't believe that the Word of God [meaning the King James Version] is true and *perfect*, like God promised to preserve it … then you have absolutely no business being in the ministry!" (p. 90, emphasis added).

He states the *KJV Only* position in his *Introduction*: "We believe that the Bible [the KJV] is the Word of God, and we also believe that God has preserved it **perfect** for us today.

"It was not just perfect in the original autograph [by that he means the original, inspired manuscripts]" (p. 7, emphasis added).

Burton thinks that every Christian should make the following confession about the King James Bible: "This Book is the Word of God. It is true! I can trust it. It's perfect; **there are no mistakes in it**. Thank God for His Word!" (Page 7, emphasis added).

No Scribal Errors or Mistranslations?

To claim that the 1611 KJV is absolutely without error, that no scribal mistakes or translator imperfections exist in it can be proven false from the King James Bible itself!

That was a statement based on wishful thinking alone — not on honest observations. As we'll soon see, the obvious, proven facts show otherwise. You don't *honor* something by making false claims about it! And you don't have to be a used-car salesman to sell us a bill of goods for the Bible

Let's Examine the Plain Facts!

Let's look into a few of these scribal inconsistencies. (You can check these out for yourself.) *Blind faith* is okay, but it's

far better to base your convictions on absolute and undeniable *facts*. Jumping to conclusions without any basis in *fact* either shows immaturity or downright dishonesty!

Taking Scripture Out of Context

Unfortunately *KJV Only* advocates have a habit of taking Scripture verses out of context and giving them their own twist. For example, what some texts say about the *Word of God*, they make them read "*the 1611 KJV.*"

To illustrate: "The Word of God is perfect" has come to mean "the *King James Version* is perfect." That "God *preserves* His Word forever" means: "*God has and will preserve the KJV forever flawless and without error.*" That's their take on it.

Forget about the facts! Forget about obvious scribal errors! Forget about mistranslations! — "The KJV has no errors. Period!"

"It's the only version that's absolutely error-free!" they would have you believe. "And if you know what's good for you, you'd better shut your eyes to the obvious — or anathema on you!"

"...The Lord is very <u>pitiful</u>..."

James 5:11

(extremely compassionate)

Numerical Inconsistencies

Now, what are the *real* facts? The Bible contains several parallel passages where the historical accounts are repeated almost word-for-word in another section of the Bible. This is especially true in the Old Testament.

Those who insist there are <u>no</u> scribal errors or mistranslations in the KJV are hard-pressed to explain the existence of these numerical inconsistencies. But all of them are easily verifiable by anyone taking the time to do so.

In the Hebrew language particularly, numbers were easily misread by translators — especially those who weren't absolutely fluent in the original languages.

The following list includes some of these more obvious *numerical errors*. These are not meant to belittle the King James Bible by any means.

As stated before, I have a very high regard and appreciation for this classic version of the Bible. And it certainly doesn't need to be girded up with *false* or *fictitious* claims.

Neither should its *presumed* perfection be used as a hatchet to chop to pieces some of the more historically accurate versions.

Solomon's Forty Thousand Stalls of Horses

"And Solomon had *forty thousand* stalls of horses for his chariots, and twelve thousand horsemen" (1 Kings 4:26).

Compare this with the following: "And Solomon had *four thousand* stalls for horses and chariots and twelve thousand horsemen" (2 Chronicles 9:25).

Why this difference of 36,000 stalls? More likely than not, a *mistranslation*.

How High Were the Two Pillars of Brass?

"For he [Hiram of Tyre] cast two pillars of brass, of *eighteen cubits high apiece*..." (1 Kings 7:15).

Compare this with the following passage: "Also he [Hiram of Tyre] made before the house two pillars of *thirty and five* cubits high..." (2 Chronicles 3:15) — a difference in height of 17 cubits!

This second passage is obviously speaking of the same person, Hiram of Tyre [although it uses an alternate spelling — *Huram*] (see 2 Chronicles 2:11).

How Many Chief Officers Did Solomon Appoint?

"These were the chief of the officers that were over Solomon's work, *five hundred and fifty*, who bore rule over the people who wrought in the work" (I Kings 9:23).

Compare this with the following parallel passage: "And these were the chief of King Solomon's officers, even *two hundred and fifty*, who bore rule over the people" (2 Chronicles 8:10).

A difference of three hundred chiefs!

How Many Baths Did Solomon's Temple Contain?

"It contained *two thousand* baths" (1 Kings 7:26), compared with: "And [the temple] held *three thousand* baths" (2 Chronicles 4:5) — a difference of 1,000 baths.

How Many Years of Famine Did the Prophet Gad Predict?

"So Gad came to David and told him and said unto him, Shall *seven* years of famine come unto thee in thy land…?" (2 Samuel 24:13), compared with: "So Gad came to David, and said unto him: Thus saith the Lord, Choose for thyself: Either *three years* of famine…" (1 Chronicles 21:11-12) — a difference of four years.

An 84 Million Dollar Error?

"And they came to Ophir, and fetched from thence gold, *four hundred and twenty talents*, and brought it to King Solomon" (1 Kings 9:28). Compare: "…And they went with the servants of Solomon to Opher, and took thence *four hundred and fifty talents of gold*, and brought them to King Solomon" (2 Chronicles 8:18) — only a difference of 30 talents?

So what's the big deal? What's the value of 30 talents of gold? Over $84 million dollars today! (Talent = 114 lbs. x 16 oz. = 1,824 oz. x $1,540+ [average price per ounce today] = $2,808,960 per talent x 30 talents = $84,268,800). Not exactly chicken scratch if you ask me!

Easy Mistakes to Make

All of the above examples are instances of mistranslations of Hebrew numbers — easy mistakes to make.

They're insignificant errors as far as doctrine goes, and should not detract from the immense value of the King James Version to the English-speaking people of the world.

We point them out merely to show that the *KJV Only* position is proven false upon evidence from the Bible itself. And we'll discuss a little later why their unfounded claims are a potential hazard to the Body of Christ.

Scribal Errors in the New Testament

We also find scribal inconsistencies in the New Testament. For example, the following passage in the KJV, which is the account of Jesus casting out demons in the country of the Gadarenes, reads:

"There met him two possessed with devils, coming out of the tombs, exceedingly fierce, that no man might pass by that way" (Matthew 8:28). Verse 29 continues to refer to the *two* men by using the plural forms, "they…we…us."

"And they went out into the fields, and gathered their vineyards, and <u>trode</u> the grapes, and made merry..."

Judges 9:27

(pressed, stomped into juice)

If we compare this story with the parallel passages in Mark and Luke, they report only **one** demon-possessed man — not two (Mark 5:1-16; Luke 8:26-36). This was obviously a scribal copying error.

So what do *KJV Only* advocates say about this and the other numerical inconsistencies? *Nothing*! (At least I haven't seen any of their attempts to get around the differences in these parallel passages.)

The Account of Saul's Conversion

Although this isn't exactly a numerical inconsistency, it's another instance of a scribal oversight in the New Testament.

Speaking of Saul's conversion, the KJV reads: "And the men who journeyed with him stood speechless, *hearing a voice*, but seeing no man" (Acts 9:7).

Compare that with Paul's retelling of the story later on: "And they that were with me saw indeed the light and were afraid; but they *heard not the voice* of him that spoke to me" (Acts 22:9; 26:14).

You can't have it both ways! Either they heard the voice or they didn't. Which was it?

Of course, Dr. C.J. Scofield, whom the *KJV Only* people condemn vehemently, comes to their defense in his footnote to Acts 9:7. He says:

"A contradiction has been imagined. The three statements should be taken together [Acts 9:7; 22:9; 26:14]. The men heard the "voice" as a sound (Gk *phonē*) but did not hear the "voice" as articulating the words, 'Saul, Saul," etc."

Good try, Dr. Scofield! The *KJV Only* bunch should stop bashing you and start *applauding* you!

Are the KJV Only People Right in Claiming Error-Free Perfection?

If the KJV is 100% error-free — as the *KJV Only* apologists insist, how could it contain these numerical errors? How is it that these parallel passages don't harmonize? How could one passage say 4,000 stalls, and a corresponding passage say 40,000? (II Chronicles 9:25; 1 Kings 4:26).

"...and did let none of his words <u>fall</u> <u>to</u> <u>the</u> <u>ground</u>."

1 Sam. 3:19

(His words were heard by the people.)

You Can't Have Your Cake and Eat it Too!

In order to maintain their rigid position, the *KJV Only* defenders have to say they're *both right* (even though one of them is obviously wrong). Can you guess which one is wrong?

The *KJV Only* bunch! That's whose wrong! And the facts prove it!

Even if there was only one instance of parallel passages in conflict, that would be enough to discount their claims. But there are many such instances.

The Inerrancy of the Original Inspired Manuscripts

Now let's look at some other instances of scribal oversight or mistranslations that have found their way into the King James Version. These should not in any way detract from the inerrancy of the original inspired manuscripts, but they do point out the human imperfections of well-meaning scribes and less-than-perfect translators.

"And he will appoint him captains over thousands…and will set them to <u>ear</u> his ground…"

1 Sam. 8:12

(to cultivate)

A Kab of Dove's Dung

The following passage has a provocative reading: "…and the fourth part of a kab of *dove's dung* for five pieces of silver" (2 Kings 6:25).

Somewhere along the line, a translator mistook a similar-looking Hebrew word, meaning a vegetable (possibly seed pods) for *dove's dung*.

The setting of this passage was the siege of Samaria by Syria, causing a great famine. Dove's dung may have been useful for fertilizer, but what was in great demand at the moment was something edible — a vegetable from which they could make a salad or stew (Strong's #2755, 2nd definition).

Thou Hast **Not** Increased Their Joy

Let's take a look at this verse in Isaiah: "Thou hast multiplied the nation, and **not** increased the joy" (Isaiah 9:3).

Try as you may, you won't find the word "*not*" in the Hebrew text. (We checked it out in the Hebrew Masoretic Text, which is what the *KJV Only* gang swears by.)

"...coming down from the high place with a <u>psaltery</u> and a <u>tabret</u>, and a <u>pipe</u>, and a <u>harp</u>..."

1 Sam. 10:5

(lyre, tambourine, flute)

Why? Because it's not there! So how did it get into the KJV Bible? This mistranslation gave the text the exact opposite meaning. It should read: "…and *increased* the joy."

No mistakes in the KJV? Who's kidding who?

Why can't they accept it for what the King James Translation Committee itself intended: "*A translation to correct previous errors and an attempt to compare available translations and utilize the most reliable manuscripts available.*"

Is the Brother of John James or Jacob?

The first four verses of Acts 12 have two major translation problems in the King James Bible. The first is in verse 2, where the translators refer to *James*, the brother of John, whom King Herod had killed (Acts 12:2).

The Greek *Textus Receptus* (or Received Text), which the *KJV Only* gang *love* to love, shows his name as *Iakobos*, which is *Jacob* in English — not *James* (Strong's #2385).

When the text refers to the *Jacob* of the Old Testament, they've correctly translated it "*Jacob*," but all the other times they've mistranslated it "*James*."

This held true for James the Apostle and the other occasions were *Jacob* would have been the correct reading (Matthew 10:3; Mark 15:40; Luke 6:16; Acts 1:13; Acts 12:7).

(Unger's Bible Dictionary says that all these references to *James* should be *Jacōbus*.)

In Spanish, as well as in most other languages, the translators got it right. They correctly use the name *Jacobo* (Jacob).

But somewhere down the line, the English translators switched the name to <u>*James*</u>. Why? Do you suppose some high-ranking English potentate way back when, with a super-inflated ego, had enough political clout to get his name memorialized in the Bible? *Just wondering*.

Of course, most of the modern versions have gone right along with the KJV name-switch and carried on the *James* tradition — **intentionally**!

Simply because the KJV translation team chose to switch names, does that make it right? How can they still claim that the 1611 translation is *without a single error*? As I said before, this sort of false witnessing doesn't do the King James Version any favors — if anything, it *dishonors* it. So why do they do it?

The Origin of Easter

A second problem we find in the 12th chapter of Acts is that the King James Version translators substituted the word "*Easter*" for *Passover* (Acts 12:4). Although this is the only time they did it, *once* is one time too many. The Greek text definitely says Pasha (Passover). *Vine's Complete Expository Dictionary* calls it a *mistranslation*. They explain:

The term "Easter" is not of Christian origin. It is another form as *Astarte*, one of the titles of the Chaldean goddess, the queen of heaven.

The pagan festival of "Easter" was quite distinct [from the Feast of Passover], and was introduced into the apostate Western religion, as part of the attempt to adapt pagan festivals to Christianity (p. 192).

The New International Version (NIV) and most of the other newer version have chosen to use the proper word — *Passover*.

Were the KJV translators *inspired* to change *Passover* to a festival of pagan origin? What do you think?

Was this simply an oversight? Or was it an intentional corruption of the text motivated by the political correctness of the day? (*That's just a thought.*)

The fact remains that the KJV translators, for whatever reason, departed from the *Textus Receptus* (Received Text) *without* any justification whatsoever — No excuse! No alibi! No nothing!

2 Sam. 18:23

(ran after)

CHAPTER THREE

Christ's Divine Nature

The most serious assault against modern translations of the Bible is the accusation that they're attempting to do away with the divinity of Jesus. The *KJV Only* camp charges modern translations with being in *collusion* —in a conspiracy to do away with Christ's divine nature (*gradually, of course*).

These are very serious charges. The divinity of Jesus Christ is *central* to true Christianity. Any effort to water down so essential a doctrine *should* be exposed.

The New World Translation

The *New World Translation* used by the Jehovah's Witnesses does in fact attempt to reduce Christ to a mere human status. I've heard them say that although Jesus was a good man — perhaps the best man who ever lived — he was still only a man, not God. Their Bible (the NWT) intentionally corrupts certain key texts in an effort to *neutralize* Christ's divinity.

Some of the changes are quite subtle. For example, speaking of Jesus, my Bible reads in John 1:1: "In the beginning was the Word [Logos], and the Word was with God, and the Word was God."

Here John is identifying Jesus as the *Logos*, "the Word of Creation, the divine expression, the original cause" (Strong's #3056).

What does the Jehovah's Witnesses' *New World Translation* do? It substitutes one little word — "*a*" for "*the*." By changing the *definite article* to an *indefinite article*, they have compromised the meaning, making Jesus out to be merely "*a*" word — not "*the*" *Creative Logos*. "In the beginning was the Word, and the word was with God, and the word was a god *[small g]*" (John 1:1 NWT 2013 Edition).

In one fell swoop they've succeeded in *negating* a powerful proof-text that clearly attributes divinity to Jesus Christ. They do this without manuscript support for this corruption of the text. It was done to enhance an unorthodox theological position — a heretical doctrinal error.

Are Modern Translations Also Suspect?

Are the NKJV, NIV, NLT, NASB and other modern translations also guilty of playing loose with the inspired Word of God? According to the *KJV Only* advocates — *yes*.

And when it comes to the doctrine of Christ's divine nature, there couldn't be a more serious charge. In essence, these updated versions are accused of fostering down-right heresy.

If there's any truth to these incriminating charges, then the entire Christian world *should* rise up in arms against the culprits and boycott their products.

What Kind of Weapons?

What ammunition does the *KJV Only* camp deploy against these popular modern translations? Their biggest assault is that "these Johnny-come-lately translations have deleted dozens of references to Jesus." Why would modern translation do such a despicable thing? "*Because there's a conspiracy*," they tell us, "*to down-play Christ's divinity*."

2 Kings 6:25

(a measure of a kind of vegetable)

Ignoring the Obvious

Of course, the obvious reason for these deletions is ignored — or discredited. Since the time that the KJV was first published, over 400 years ago, hundreds of ancient and authentic manuscripts have been unearthed. Some of them are many centuries closer to the time of Christ. The Dead Sea Scrolls were discovered in a cave at Qumran in 1947.

These, as well as other finds in the vicinity, predate the previously available manuscripts by as much as 1,000 years. In fact, some of these scrolls were written during the first half of the first century AD (The Concise Columbia Encyclopedia, Columbia University Press, NY, 1983, p. 222).

It's generally accepted knowledge that the closer in time one comes to the original (the older ones), the more reliable a manuscript copy tends to be. More recent manuscripts are less likely to be as true-to-form.

Expansion of Piety

So, why do we sometimes see words like "*Jesus*" in the KJV, but not in others? One reason is that *pious copyists* (men

prompted by their piety) occasionally took the liberty to *expand* the manuscript text.

It worked like this: In cases where a personal pronoun referring to deity was used, such as "*he*" or "*him*," when copying the manuscript, they would sometimes replace it with the name "Jesus" or "Jesus Christ," etc.

I'm sure they meant no harm by it. In fact, they probably did it to avoid any ambiguity. This is referred to as *expansion of piety*. This means that "additions have been made to the text that flow from a desire to protect and reverence divine truths" (The King James Only Controversy, by James R. White, Bethany House Publishers, Minn. MN ©1995, p. 43).

All Scripture Inspired

Modern translators have chosen to use the more ancient and reliable manuscripts over the more recent "*expanded*" ones. This action was based on their conviction that the "*original autographs*" (original scrolls) were *verbally inspired*.

The basis of their belief is 2 Timothy 3:16 and 2 Peter 1:21: "All Scripture is given by inspiration of God …" (2 Timothy 3:16).

"For the prophecy came not in old time by the will of man: but holy men of God spake as they were moved by the Holy Ghost" (2 Peter 1:21).

Any omissions of the names of deity in the modern versions were prompted by a desire to be *true* to those more ancient and authentic manuscripts, and not due to some sinister plot to cast doubt on the divine attributes of the Lord Jesus.

Some of the accusations of *conspiracy* leveled against these updated translations appear to be more emotional hemorrhaging than an unbiased review of the facts.

Instead of using the more ancient and reliable manuscripts as a yard-stick, their detractors have propped up the KJV as the *standard*, and judge all other translations by how they *align* themselves with it — or how they *deviate* from it.

In some circles, the controversy has reached a pitch of near hysteria. Forget about the clear facts. Forget about the *Dead Sea Scrolls*. Forget about the other discoveries that predate the Byzantine texts (from which the KJV was derived) by a thousand years. Forget about the God-given blessings of having biblical resources so much more authentic and trustworthy

today than what was available 400 years ago. *"If it's not KJV,"* they insist, *"it's not the real thing!"*

A Baseless Charge?

So what about the charge that *"these modern translations are trying to do away with the teaching that Jesus is God?"* Is there any truth to it? Is there really a basis for these *"conspiracy"* charges? Or is the truth elsewhere? If anything, the evidence shows just the opposite! For the sake of honesty, let's take a closer look.

Believe it or not, there are modern translations that actually strengthen the doctrine of Christ's divinity, as compared to the KJV.

The Only Begotten Son

Take for example John 1:18. This is one of those "key" passages regarding the deity of Jesus Christ. Here's how the KJV reads: "No man hath seen God at any time; **the only begotten Son**, which is in the bosom of the Father, he hath declared to him."

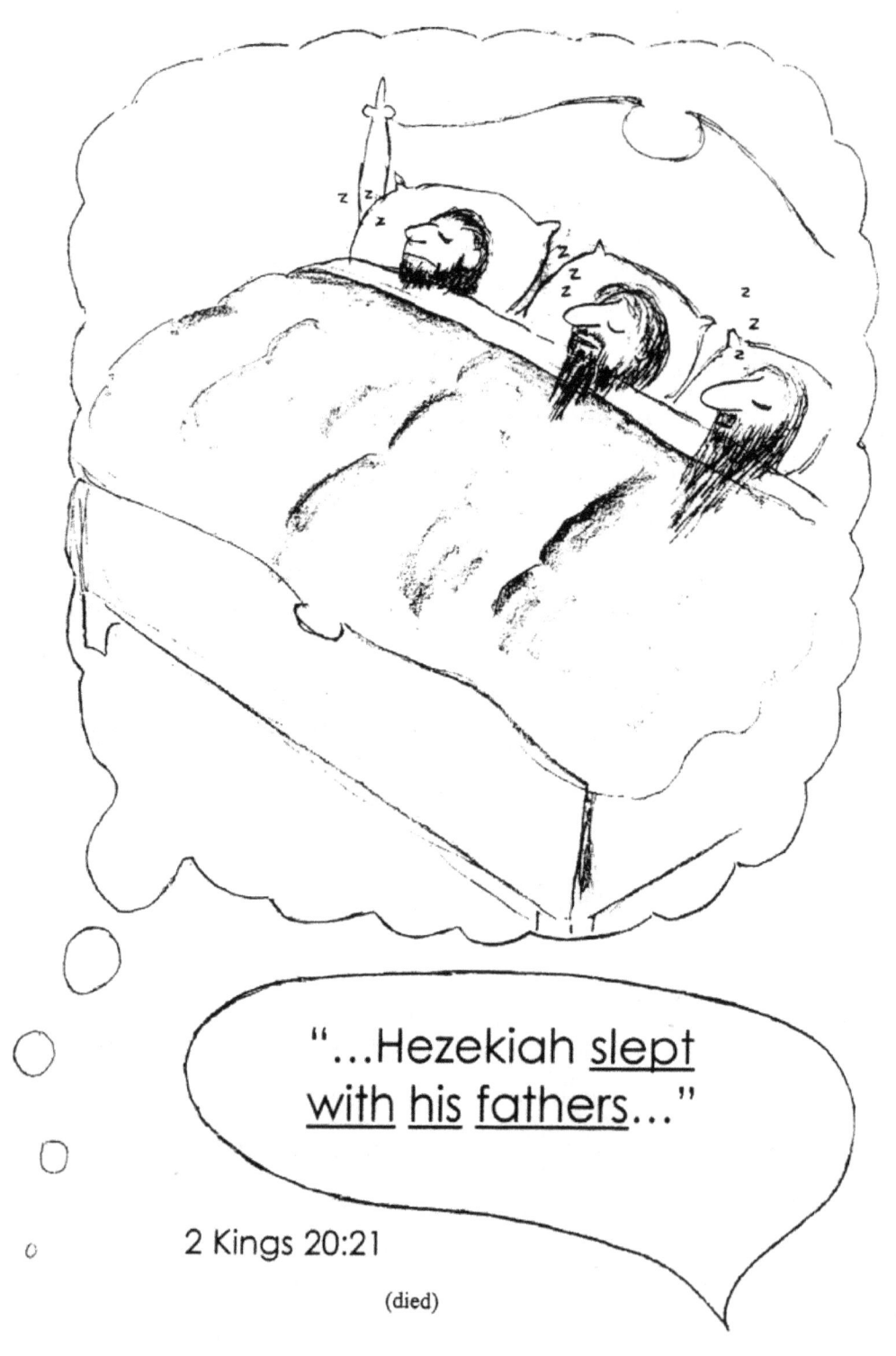

When it comes to affirming the divine nature of Jesus Christ, how do the modern translations compare? How do these "key" words in the KJV stack up with more modern updated versions?

KJV: The **only begotten Son**

NASB: The **only begotten God**

NIV: **God the One and Only**

NRSV: It is **God the Only Son**

Here we see that the KJV has no clear reference to the divine nature of Jesus Christ, whereas the NASB, NIV, and NRSV unmistakably identify Him as God. Actually, other than calling Him the Son of God, the KJV doesn't even identify Him as God.

Did the scholars who gave us the KJV have an agenda to minimize Christ's deity in this text? Of course not! If anything, the *KJV Only* camp should applaud these modern renderings as more precisely enunciating the doctrine of Christ's divine nature. (But don't hold your breath.)

These alternate renderings are supported by an abundance of manuscript evidence far more authentic than the Textus Receptus used by the KJV (Ibid. pp. 198-200).

"The two pillars, one <u>sea</u>, and the <u>bases</u> which Solomon had made for the house of the Lord; the brass of all these vessels was <u>without weight</u>."

2 Kings 25:16

(temple laver, foundations *or* stands, more than could be weighed)

We're convinced that the KJV scholars *for the most part* did the best they could with the resources at their disposal. But since then, God, in His sovereignty, has allowed archaeologists to make some spectacular finds of manuscripts so priceless, ancient and authentic as to revitalize biblical scholarship.

Rather than suppressing the evidence brought to light, we should be deeply thankful and eternally grateful to our Heavenly Father. And instead of assuming that the KJV is the *standard*, we need to acknowledge that its sources were *limited* by the lack of manuscript evidence available to us today.

Denying the Only True God

Consider another passage which is *key* to understanding the deity of Jesus Christ. Jude, verse 4, talks about those who deny the Lord. The KJV reads: "…denying **the only Lord God, and our Lord Jesus Christ**."

At first glance, it looks as though it's speaking about two personages: God *and* Jesus. This is due in part to the way the sentence is structured, and in part to the addition of the word "God" in the text.

Updated translations render the pertinent portion of the text: "…and deny **our only Master and Lord, Jesus Christ**" (NASB). This rendering makes it clear that the text is speaking of only *one* person, Jesus Christ, who is both *Lord* and *Master*.

There's no guessing at the meaning here. It's a clear-sounding testimony to the divinity of the Lord Jesus. It's obviously not separating Jesus from God (as the KJV appears to do). And it's also attributing *full divinity* to Jesus Christ!

Did the KJV translating committee have a vendetta against identifying Christ as God? Of course not! And these updated translations don't either. Just the opposite is true!

Fullness of the Godhead

One of the best-known *proof texts* about Christ's true nature is Colossians 2:9. The KJV reads: "For in him dwelleth all the fullness of the **Godhead** bodily."

If you were trying to explain the term "Godhead" to an unchurched person unfamiliar with Christian terms, what would you tell him? What does "Godhead" mean in our current vernacular? A giant carved head of God? — Sort of like the

heads of presidents chiseled in stone on Mount Rushmore?

Of course, to those of us who have been brought up in church, we know it to be a reference to the Trinity, made up of the three divine personages — Father, Son and Holy Spirit. But for the average Joe Blow, the word "*Godhead*" needs some explaining.

On the other hand, almost everyone knows that "*divine*" and "*deity*" have to do with the nature of God, or with God Himself. The updated translations are explicitly clear that the text is acknowledging the divinity of Christ: "For Him all the fullness of **deity** dwells in bodily form" (Colossians 2:9 NASB). This is a concise and resounding witness to the fact that Jesus Christ is God revealed in human form.

No, there's no collusion to abolish the divinity of Jesus Christ here.

Sanctify the Lord God

An effective way to deal with Jehovah's Witnesses is to show how the New Testament refers to Jesus as the *Yahweh* of the Old Testament.

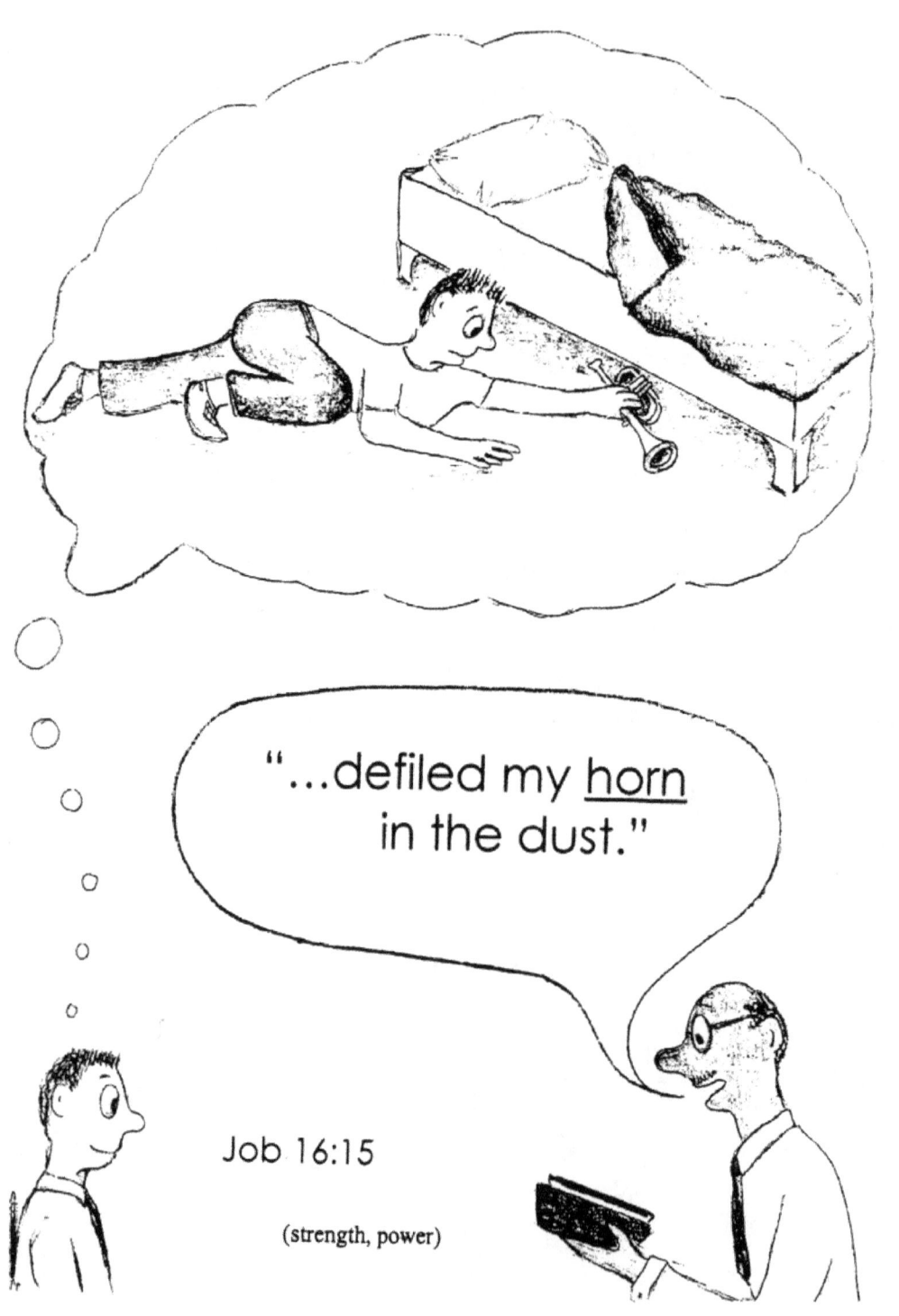

I Peter 3:15 offers a perfect example. Here, Peter quotes from a passage in Isaiah which states in part: "Sanctify the **Lord of hosts** himself…" (Isaiah 8:12-13). ["Lord" is how the KJV translates "Jehovah" (Yahweh, the self-Existent or Eternal — Strong's #3068]).

However, in citing this passage from Isaiah, Peter substitutes *"**Christ as Lord**"* for *"**Lord** [Jehovah] **of Hosts**,"* thereby affirming Christ's identity with the Old Testament "**Lord**" (*Yahweh*).

Unfortunately, the impact is lost in the KJV translation. Here are how the different versions of 1 Peter 3:15 compare:

KJV: Sanctify **the Lord God**

NRSV: Sanctify **Christ as Lord**

NIV: Set apart **Christ as Lord**

NLT: Worship **Christ as Lord** of your life

When it comes to affirming the deity of Christ, of the four translations, the KJV is the weakest. In fact, the KJV doesn't even mention Christ.

The other three versions specifically refer to Christ as **Lord**, (literally supreme, also translated as God) — (Strong's #2962, kurios).

In relying on the less-authentic *Textus Receptus*, which uses "*Lord God*" instead of "*Christ as Lord*," the KJV translators have unwittingly missed this dynamic witness to the deity of Christ.

In so doing, they had to ignore overwhelming manuscript evidence that gives support to the divine nature of Christ.

I'm sure, if the tables were turned, there would be loud shouts of "*treason*" against the modern versions. But since it's *their* translation that has short-changed us, the *KJV Only* camp remains silent. I wonder why!

Did the KJV translation committee have some kind of agenda to downplay Christ's deity? Of course not! But neither is there a conspiracy among the updated translations.

We could go on, citing other instances where the KJV translators have obscured the meaning due to their adherence to less reliable sources — instance where up-to-date translations give a resounding testimony to the divinity of the Lord Jesus.

"...by reason of <u>breakings</u> they <u>purify</u> themselves."

Job 41:25

(They are terrified by the crashing noises.)

Our Recommendation

For those who are interested in a more comprehensive study, we wholeheartedly recommend an excellent resource. It's a wealth of information, not only for the deity of Christ, but also for manuscript sources and the whole *KJV Only* issue.

We're referring to James R. White's book, *The King James Only Controversy*, (Bethany House Publishing, © 1995, Minn. MN)

CHAPTER FOUR

Selected Archaisms

According to Nehemiah 8:8, God's Word should be *clear*, *distinct* and *understandable*! That makes sense, doesn't it? Most of the KJV Bible's language is understandable. It's still considered a classic in prose and poetic symmetry. This is not a plea to replace it with any of the *up-to-date versions*.

However, should the Lord delay His return for another 100 years, the KJV will have gone the way of the *Latin Vulgate* and the Old English Bishop's Bible. How many today would choose the reading of Old English poet Chaucer's "*The Canterbury Tales*" as their preferred form of recreation?

Just a Sampling of Archaisms

The following list of *King James Version* **archaisms** is by no means all-inclusive. It's merely a sampling found throughout the 66 books of the KJV Bible. Some are so strange-sounding that they're guaranteed to make you smile. They may even provoke a chuckle.

The cartoons were created by co-author, Sonya Carlson. She's done a superb job of catching some of the humor inspired by these *archaic* expressions.

The *purpose* of this list is obvious — to emphasize the importance of up-to-date translations — versions that give a clearer and more precise meaning to the heavenly message. As we've said before, the very words of Scripture are inspired — as *originally given*.

As pointed out in Nehemiah 8:8, the Written Word should be *clear*, *distinct*, and *readily understood*. Unfortunately, this is not always the case with the *King James Version*.

Why Words and Meanings Change

After all, the KJV was translated over 400 years ago, and languages do have a way of evolving. Even in our own generation we've seen thousands upon thousands of new words added to our vocabulary. Other words, such as *gay*, *pitiful*, *carelessly*, *prevent*, *awful* and *careful*, now have entirely different meanings than they did when the KJV was first published.

"He that hateth gifts shall live..."

Prov. 15:27

(bribes)

How To Use The Following List

In the list that follows, right after the Scripture reference, the obsolete word or archaic phrase is highlighted in **bold letters**. It is followed by its most commonly accepted meaning which is *italicized* and in (parenthesis). We've listed 715 of them.

To test your skill in understanding *King James English*, have someone read you the archaic phrase and see if you can come up with a corresponding meaning. (Even ministers who've been bottle-fed on the *King James Version* since childhood sometimes miss a few of them.)

Better still, run some of these archaisms by your neighborhood teenagers — especially if they're unchurched. See how well they do.

If you get 50% (375 of them or less, you're considered KJV illiterate. 70% (500 of them) is passing. If you get 80% (575 or more), you're suspect of being a KJV Only zealot. Have fun!

Selected King James Version Archaisms

Gen. 8:1	and the waters **asswaged** (the waters *subsided*, or *receded*).
Gen. 18:12	After I am **waxed** old (after I have *become old*, or *worn out*).
Gen. 18:24	**Peradventure** there are fifty (*Suppose*; or *what if* there are fifty).
Gen. 19:9	they **pressed sore** upon the man (they kept *bringing pressure* on the man).
Gen. 22:3	**clave** the wood for the…offering (*cut* wood for the…offering).
Gen. 24:25	we have both straw and **provender** (plenty of straw and *fodder*).
Gen. 25:29	Jacob **sod pottage** (Jacob was *cooking some stew*).
Gen. 26:8	Isaac was **sporting** with Rebekah (was *laughing* with Rebekah).
Gen. 26:31	They rose up **betimes** in the morning (*early the next morning*).
Gen. 28:11	he **lighted upon** a certain place (when he *reached* a certain place).
Gen. 30:35	the **he-goats** that were **ring-straked** (the *male goats* that were *streaked* or *spotted*).
Gen. 31:30	thou **sore longest after** thy father's house (you *longed to return* to your father's house).
Gen. 31:34	put them in the camel's **furniture** (inside her camel's *saddle*).
Gen. 31:36	Jacob…**chode** with Laban (was *angry* and *took Laban to task*).
Gen. 32:31	he **halted upon his thigh** (he was *limping* because of his hip).
Gen. 36:15	these were the **dukes** of the sons of Esau (these were the *chiefs*; or *heads* descended from Esau).

Gen. 39:8	my master **wotteth not** what is with me (*with me in charge, my master does not concern himself*).
Gen. 41:2	well favored **kine** (sleek and fat *cows*)
Gen 41:7	seven **rank**…ears (seven *healthy, full heads* of grain).
Gen. 43:1	the famine was **sore** (the famine was *severe*)
Gen. 43:7	the man asked us **straitly** of our state (*carefully, specifically*)
Gen. 43:30	for **his bowels did yearn** upon [him] (he was *deeply moved*).
Gen. 43:34	Benjamin's **mess** was five times so much as any of theirs (Benjamin's reward was five times as much as anyone else's)
Gen. 48:14	guiding his hands **wittingly** (guiding his hands *knowingly*).
Gen. 49:27	Benjamin shall **ravin** as a wolf (Benjamin is a ravenous wolf).
Gen. 49:33	he **gathered up his feet** into the bed (he *went to bed to die*).
Gen. 49:33	and **yielded up the ghost** (and *breathed his last*).
Gen. 50:1	Joseph **fell upon his father's face** (*emotionally embraced him*)
Exo. 1:10	when **there falleth out any war** (if *war breaks out*).
Exo. 2:3	she laid [the ark] in the **flags** by the river's brink (in the *reeds* along the river's bank).
Exo. 2:4	his sister stood afar off to **wit** what would be done to him (*to see*).
Exo. 3:5	draw not **nigh hither** (Do not come *any closer*).
Exo. 3:22	ye shall **spoil** the Egyptians (you will *plunder* the Egyptians.)
Exo. 5:8	the **tale** of the bricks (the *number* of the bricks)

Exo. 5:19	ye shall not **minish** ought from your bricks (*you are not to reduce the number* of bricks required of you for each day.)	
Exo. 5:21	ye have made our **savour to be abhorred** (you have made us *offensive*, or a *stench*.)	
Exo. 7:15	stand by the river's brink **against he come** (*to meet him*.)	
Exo. 8:9	Moses said unto Pharaoh, **glory over me** (*command me*, or, *I leave to you the favor of setting the time*.)	
Exo. 8:22	I will **sever**…the land of Goshen (I will *set apart* to deal kindly with, or *deal differently* with the land of Goshen.)	
Exo. 9:3	there shall be a very **grievous murrain** (*a terrible plague*)	
Exo. 9:9	a boil breaking forth with **blains** (*ulcers*, or *festering boils*)	
Exo. 12:9	Eat not of it raw, nor **sodden** at all with water (*cooked* in water)	
Exo. 12:9	with the **purtenance** thereof (with *the inward parts*)	
Exo. 13:12	that openeth the **matrix** (who opens the *womb*, or every *firstborn*)	
Exo. 13:16	for **frontlets** between thine eyes (*a symbol on your forehead*)	
Exo. 13:18	the children of Israel went up **harnessed** (*armed for battle*)	
Exo. 16:4	gather a certain **rate** every day (gather *enough* for that day)	
Exo. 16:14	as small as the **hoar frost** (*thin flakes like frost*)	
Exo. 16:18	they did **mete it with an omer** (they *measured it by the omer*)	
Exo. 16:23	and **seethe that ye will seethe** (*boil what you want to boil*)	
Exo. 17:13	Joshua **discomfited** Amalek (*overcame* the Amalekite army)	

Exo. 19:17	they stood at the **nether** part of the mount (at the *foot of the mountain*)
Exo. 21:19	Then shall he that smote him be **quit** (be *cleared of charges*)
Exo. 22:29	offer the first of thy **liquors** (the *overflow of your vats*, or do not hold back the *offerings from your vats*)
Exo. 22:30	seven days [shall thy sheep] be with his **dam** (Let them *stay with their mother* for seven days)
Exo. 23:2	neither shalt thou speak in a cause to **decline after many to wrest justice.** (*Do not prevent justice by siding with the crowd.*)
Exo. 23:3	neither shalt thou **countenance a poor man** (do not show *favoritism against a poor man* in his lawsuit)
Exo. 23:8	Thou shalt take no **gift** (Do not accept a *bribe*)
Exo. 25:31	its **knops** and its flowers (its *flower-like cups*)
Exo. 26:6	Thou shalt make fifty **taches** (*gold clasps*)
Exo. 27:4	Thou shalt make four **brazen** rings (*bronze* rings)
Exo. 27:17	the pillars…shall be **filleted** with silver (shall be *banded*)
Exo. 28:8	the **curious girdle** of the ephod (*skillfully woven belt*)
Exo. 28:9	**grave** on them the names (*engrave* on them)
Exo. 28:11	make them to be set in **ouches** of gold (in gold *filigree settings*)
Exo. 28:4	fasten the **wreathen** chains to the **ouches** (attach the *braided* chains to the *settings*)

Exo. 28:32	as it were the hole of an **habergeon** (a *coat of mail*, or a *collar*)
Exo. 29:9	put the **bonnets** on (put *turbans*, or *headbands* on)
Exo. 29:13	the **caul** that is above the liver (the *fat* covering of the liver)
Exo. 29:27	which is…**heaved up** (that was *lifted high*, or *presented*)
Exo. 30:4	for the **staves to bear it withal** (for the *poles to carry it*)
Exo. 30:35	a **confection** after the art of the **apothecary** (a *fragrant blend of incense*, the work of a *perfumer*)
Exo. 31:4	to **devise cunning works** (to *make artistic designs*)
Exo. 31:6	all that are **wisehearted** (all the *skilled craftsmen*)
Exo. 32:20	**strawed** it upon the water (*scattered* it on the water)
Exo. 32:23	**we wot not** (*we don't know*)
Exo. 34:15	they **go a whoring** after their gods (the *play the harlot* or *prostitute themselves*)
Exo. 34:17	Thou shalt make thee no **molten gods** (Do not make *cast idols*)
Exo. 36:20	**shittim wood** (*acacia wood*)
Exo. 37:22	their **knops** and their branches (the *buds* and the branches)
Exo. 38:28	overlaid their **chapiters** and **filleted** them (to overlay the *tops of the posts* and to *make their bands*)
Lev. 5:1	hear the voice of **swearing** (*speaking a curse* on someone)
Lev. 7:9	all that is **dressed** in the frying pan (*prepared* in a pan)
Lev. 11:18	the **gier** eagle (the *carrion eagle*, or *osprey*)
Lev. 13:10	**quick** raw flesh in the **rising** (*raw flesh in the swelling*)

Lev. 13:31	the plague of the **scall** (a plague of *scabby eruptions*, or a *sore of an infection*)
Lev. 13:52	a **fretting** leprosy (a *festering* leprosy, or *contamination of destructive mildew*)
Lev. 25:5	Neither gather the grapes of thy vine **undressed** (*unpruned* or *untended vines*)
Lev. 25:25	if thy brother be **waxen poor** (if one of your countrymen *becomes poor*)
Lev. 25:27	restore the **overplus** (the *overpayment* or *refund* the balance)
Lev. 25:35	if thy brother be…**fallen in decay with thee** (if one of your countrymen is unable to support himself or fails financially)
Num. 1:18	they declared their **pedigrees** (they revealed their *lineages*)
Num. 2:34	they **pitched** by their standards (they *encamped* under their standards)
Num. 7:19	one silver **charger** (one *platter* or *plate*)
Num. 10:21	[they] set up the tabernacle **against they came** (*before they arrived*)
Num. 11:30	Moses **gat** him into the camp (Moses *returned* to the camp.)

Num. 16:30	they go down **quick** into the pit (go down *alive* into the *grave*)
Num. 20:3	the people **chode** with Moses (*quarreled* with Moses)
Num. 33:52	destroy all their **pictures** (destroy all their *stone idols* or *carved images*)
Nom. 33:52	and **quite pluck down** their high places (and *demolish* all their high places)
Deut. 1:12	how can I myself alone bear your **cumbrance** (your *problems*)
Deut. 2:14	the **space** in which we came from (*from the time we left*)
Deut. 2:14	Men of war were **wasted out** (fighting men had *perished*)
Deut. 3:18	all who are **meet** for war (all who are *fit* for war or all your *able-bodied men*)
Deut. 4:34	hath **God assayed** to go (has *any god ever tried* to take for himself one nation out of another nation?)
Deut. 4:41	Moses **severed** three cities (Moses *set aside* three cities)
Deut. 7:5	cut down their **groves** (cut down their *idols*)
Deut. 14:5	the **pygarg**…and the **chamois** (*antelope, mountain sheep*)
Deut. 14:7	the **coney**…**glede**…**lapwing** (the *rock badger, buzzard, hoopoe* (Deut. 14:7-18)
Deut. 14:21	thou shalt not **seethe** a kid (Do not *cook* a young goat in its mother's milk)
Deut. 17:1	any evil **favoredness** (that has any *defect*)

Deut. 18:3	the maw (the *stomach* or *inner parts*)
Deut. 19:18	the judges shall make **inquisition** (judges shall make a *thorough investigation*)
Deut. 21:3	hath **not been wrought with** (has *never been worked*)
Deut. 21:12	to **pare** her nails (*trim* her nails)
Deut. 22:7	let the **dam** go (let the *mother-bird* go)
Deut. 22:8	Make a **battlement** for thy roof (a *parapet* around your roof)
Deut. 22:19	they shall **amerce** him (they shall *fine* him)
Deut. 23:13	Thou shalt have a **paddle** upon thy weapon (a *shovel* among your weapons)
Deut. 23:19	Thou shalt not lend upon **usury** (When you lend money do not *charge your brother interest*.)
Deut. 25:18	smote the **hindmost** of thee (those *at the end of the march*)
Deut. 26:8	the Lord brought us forth…with **great terribleness** (with *great terror*)
Deut. 26:17	thou hast **avouched** the Lord (you have *vowed to* the Lord)
Deut. 27:16	cursed be he who **setteth light by** his father (*dishonors*)

Deut. 28:53	in the **straitness**…of thine enemies (because of the *suffering* that your enemies *will inflict on you*)
Deut. 30:18	I **denounce** unto you this day (I *declare* to you this day…)
Deut. 32:42	from the **beginning of revenges upon** the enemy (upon *the heads of the enemy leaders*)
Deut. 33:13	the deep that **coucheth beneath** (*the deep waters that lie below*)
Josh. 1:11	Prepare **victuals** (*food supplies*; get your supplies ready)
Josh. 4:1	all the people were **clean passed over** (when the whole nation had *completely crossed over*)
Josh. 6:9	the **rereward** came after the ark (the *rear guard* followed)
Josh. 6:26	Joshua **adjured** them (Joshua *pronounced* this *solemn oath*)
Josh. 8:13	their **liers** in wait (their ambushers take up their positions)
Josh. 10:10	the Lord **discomfited** them (The Lord *routed them* or threw them into confusion)
Josh. 11:6	Thou shalt **hough** their horses (*hamstring* their horses)
Josh. 15:3	And **fetched a compass** (*turned toward* or *curved around*)
Judg. 3:22	The **haft** also went in after the blade (the *hilt of the dagger* sunk in after the blade)
Judg. 14:7	She **lay sore upon him** (she *continued to nag him*)
Judg. 16:9	he broke the **withs** as a **thread of tow** (he snapped the *cords* or thongs as easily as a *piece of string*)

Judg. 16:12	there were **liers** in wait (men were hidden in the room, *waiting*)
Judg. 18:7	they dwelt **careless** [there] (the people were *living in safety*)
Judg. 18:15	they turned **thitherward** (they turned *in there*)
Judg. 18:21	they put the **carriage** before them (pulling their *belongings* in front of them)
Judg. 19:22	certain **sons of Belial** (some *wicked men*)
Ruth 1:13	**stay for them from having husbands** (*refrain from marrying*)
Ruth 1:14	Ruth **clave** unto her (Ruth *clung* to her)
Ruth 1:18	She was **steadfastly minded** (she was *determined*)
Ruth 2:8	abide here **fast by** my maidens (stay here *with* my servant girls)
Ruth 2:14	she…was **sufficed** (she ate all the wanted and was *satisfied*)
Ruth 2:19	where **wrought** thou? (Where did you *labor, glean*, today?)
Ruth 4:4	I thought to **advertise** thee (*bring the matter to your attention*)
Ruth 4:7	a man **plucked off** his shoe (a man *took off* his shoe)
1 Sam. 1:12	Eli **marked** her mouth (*watched* or *observed* her mouth)
1 Sam. 2:13	the flesh was **in seething** with a *fleshhook of three teeth* in his hand (while the meat was *being boiled*, the servant would come with a *three-pronged fork*)

1 Sam. 3:19	and did let none of his words **fall to the ground** (*his words were heard by the people*)
1 Sam. 4:9	**quit yourselves like men** (*be men*)
1 Sam. 5:6	smote them with **emerods** (smitten with *tumors*)
1 Sam. 6:7	take two **milch kine** (two *milk cows*)
1 Sam. 6:11	the **coffer** with the mice of gold (*chest* containing gold rats)
1 Sam. 7:10	**discomfited** [the Philistines] (*threw them into panic*)
1 Sam. 8:3	his sons turned aside after **lucre** (pursued *dishonest gain*)
1 Sam. 8:12	will set them to **ear** his ground (to *cultivate* his ground)
1 Sam. 8:13	take your daughters to be **confectionaries** (*perfumers*)
1 Sam. 8:21	**rehearsed** them in the ears of the Lord (*repeated* it)
1 Sam. 9:14	Samuel came **out against** them (came *towards* them)
1 Sam. 9:26	the **spring** of the day (*daybreak, dawning of the day*)
1 Sam. 10:5	with a **tabret** (*tambourines*)
1 Sam. 13:5	they **pitched** in Michmash (they *camped* at Michmash)
1 Sam. 13:6	the men were in a **strait** (*hedged in*)
1 Sam. 13:15	Samuel…**gat himself up** (Samuel *departed*)
1 Sam. 13:19	there was no **Smith** found (no *blacksmith* found)
1 Sam. 13:20	his **share** and his **coulter** (*plowshares, mattocks*)
1 Sam. 14:6	**no restraint** to the Lord (*nothing can hinder* the Lord)

1 Sam. 14:8	we will **discover** ourselves (*let them see us*)	
1 Sam. 14:20	a very great **discomfiture** (*total confusion*)	
1 Sam. 14:24	Saul had **adjured** the people (*bound them under an oath*)	
1 Sam. 17:6	[Goliath] had a **target of brass between his shoulders** (*a bronze javelin slung on his back*)	
1 Sam. 17:40	[David] put [stones] in a **script** (in a *pouch* of his bag)	
1 Sam. 17:53	[they] **spoiled** their tents (they *plundered* their camp)	
1 Sam. 18:30	[David's] name was **much set by** (*became well known*)	
1 Sam. 19:4	his works have been **thee-ward** (have *benefited you*)	
1 Sam. 19:13	[Michal] put a pillow of goat's hair for its **bolster** (*head*)	
1 Sam. 20:12	when I have **sounded** my father (*determined his intentions*)	
1 Sam. 21:13	[David] **scrabbled** on the doors (*made marks on the door*)	
1 Sam. 24:3	Saul went in to **cover his feet** (*to relieve himself*)	
1 Sam. 24:4	David cut off the skirt of Saul's robe **privily** (stealthily)	
1 Sam. 25:22	**any that pisseth against the wall** (*any male*)	
1 Sam. 27:10	**Whither** have ye made a **road** today? (*Where did you go raiding?*)	
2 Sam. 3:10	to **translate** the kingdom (*transfer the leadership*)	
2 Sam. 5:20	the **breach** of waters (the *surging* of waters)	
2 Sam. 5:23	**fetch a compass** behind them (*make a circle* around behind)	

2 Sam. 10:6	they **stank** before David (were a *stench* in David's nostrils)
2 Sam. 14:20	**fetch about this form of speech** (to *change the situation*)
2 Sam. 17:17	a **wench** went and told them (a *servant girl*)
2 Sam. 18:23	[Ahimaaz **overran** the Cushite (*ran after* or *outran him*)
2 Sam. 22:6	the snares of death **prevented** me (*came upon me*)
2 Sam. 22:27	with the **froward** thou wilt show thyself **unsavoury** (To the *crooked* you show yourself *shrewd*.)
2 Sam. 22:31	[the Lord] is a **buckler** to all them that trust in him (*a shield*)
2 Sam. 22:46	afraid **out of their close placed** (*in their strongholds*)
2 Sam. 23:7	the man must be **fenced** with iron (*armed with an iron tool*)
1 Kings 1:1	David **gat no heat** (*could not keep warm*)
1 Kings 2:17	he will not **say thee nay** (he will *not refuse you*)
1 Kings 2:36	go not forth **thence any whither** (don't go *anywhere else*)
1 Kings 3:19	this woman **overlaid** [the child] (she *lay on top of* the child)
1 Kings 3:26	her **bowels yearned upon** her son (She was *filled with compassion* for her son.)
1 King 7:33	their **naves** and their **felloes** (the *rims, spokes* and *hubs*)
1 Kings 8:47	if they shall **bethink** themselves (*have a change of heart*)
1 Kings 9:8	every one…shall **hiss** (everyone will *scoff* and say…)
1 Kings 9:21	**levy a tribute of bondservice** (*taken for slave labor*)
1 Kings 11:1	King Solomon loved many **strange** women (*foreign* women)

1 Kings 14:3	take with thee ten…**cracknels** (*cakes*)
1 Kings 14:6	Why **feignest** thou thyself? (Why this *pretence*?)
1 Ki. 17:16	the barrel of meal **wasted not** (was *not used up*)
1 Ki. 20:29	they **pitched one over against the other** (they *camped opposite each other*)
1 Ki. 22:10	[they sat] in a **void place** (they sat at the *threshing floor*)
2 Kings 2:8	the waters were divided **hither and thither** (the water divided *to the right and to the left*)
2 Kings 2:11	and **parted them both asunder** (*separated the two of them*)
2 Kings 2:23	**little children**… mocked him (*youths*; a mistranslation of Hebrew word *na'ar*, which means young men)
2 Kings 4:38	There was a **dearth** in the land (a *famine*)
2 Kings 4:38	**seethe pottage** (*cook some stew*)
2 Kings 4:43	his **servitor** said (his *servant* asked)
2 Kings 4:43	they shall eat and shall **leave thereof** (*have some left over*)
2 Kings 6:1	the place where we dwell is **too strait** for us (*too small*)
2 Kings 6:25	a **kab of dove's dung** (*a measure of a kind of vegetable*—a mistranslation: The translators confused two similar-looking Hebrew words; one meaning *dung*, the other, *vegetables*.)
2 Kings 9:2	**look out there** Jehu (*there you will see or look for* Jehu)
2 Kings 9:26	**cast** him on the **plat** of ground (*make you pay for it* on this *plot* of ground)

2 Kings 9:30	Jezebel **painted** her face, and **tired** her head (Jezebel *put on eye makeup* and *adorned her head*.)
2 Kings 9:33	he **trode** her under foot (*trampled* her under foot)
2 Kings 10:3	**look even out** the best and **meetest** (*choose* the best and *most worthy*)
2 Kings 10:5	the **bringers up** of the children (the *guardians* of children)
2 Ki. 10:15	Jehu…**lighted on** Jehonadab (*came upon*)
2 Ki. 19:10	Let none be **wanting** (see to it that no one is *missing*)
2 Ki. 10:27	they made the house of Baal a **draught house** (a *latrine*)
2 Ki. 10:32	the Lord began to **cut Israel short** (*reduce the size of Israel*)
2 Ki. 11:15	**have her forth without the ranges** (*bring her out between the ranks*)
2 Ki. 12:10	and **told the money** (and *counted the money*)
2 Ki. 12:11	they **laid** [money] out to the carpenters (*paid* the carpenters)
2 Ki. 12:13	**snuffers** (*wick trimmers*)
2 Ki. 15:5	the king dwelt in a **several** house (lived in a *separate* house)
2 Ki. 19:26	as corn **blasted** before it be grown up (*scorched* or *dried up*)
2 Ki. 20:21	Hezekiah slept with his fathers (*died and was buried with*)
2 Ki. 22:14	Huldah, the prophetess dwelt in the **college** (*second district*)

2 Ki. 23:3	the people **stood to** the covenant (*pledged themselves*)
2 Ki. 25:1	Nebuchadnezzar **pitched against** Jerusalem (*encamped by*)
2 Ki. 25:16	the brass of all these vessels was **without weight** (*more than could be weighed*)
2 Ki. 25:17	the second pillar was made with **wreathen work** (*with its braided network*)
2 Ki. 25:27	the king did **lift up the head of** Jehoiachin (*released him from prison*)
1 Chr. 2:7	who transgressed in the **thing accursed** (*violated the ban on taking devoted things*)
1 Chr. 9:28	bring the vessels in and out by **tale** (*they counted them*)
1 Chr. 11:12	one of three **mighties** (*one of three mighty men*)
1 Chr. 13:11	the Lord had **made a breach upon** Uzza (*The Lord's wrath had broken out against Uzza.*)
1 Chr. 14:15	hear a sound of **going** (*the sound of marching*)
1 Chr. 15:13	we sought him not in the **due order** (*in the prescribed way*)
1 Chr. 16:3	David dealt to everyone a **flagon of wine** (a mistranslation— *a cake of raisins*—Strong's #809)
1 Chr. 16:41	who were **expressed** by name (*designated by name*)
1 Chr. 17:21	to make thee a **name of terribleness** (*awesome wonders*)

1 Chr. 20:3	**harrows** of iron (iron *picks*)
1 Chr. 22:5	the house must be **magnifical** (*of great magnificence*)
1 Chr. 23:6	David divided them into **courses** (into *divisions*)
1 Chr. 24:31	cast lots **over against** their brethren (*as their brothers had done*)
1 Chr. 25:8	they cast lots **ward against ward** (they cast lots *for their duties*)
1 Chr. 26:15	house of **Asuppim** (a transliteration, meaning: *the store-house*)
2 Chr. 2:2	Solomon **told out** three score and ten thousand men (*counted* or *conscripted*)
2 Chr. 3:6	he **garnished** the house (he *adorned* the temple)
2 Chr. 4:13	to cover the two **pommels** of the **chapiters** (to cover the two *bowls* of the *capitals*; *bowl-shaped capitals*)
2 Chr. 4:20	before the **oracle** of pure gold (in front of the *inner sanctuary*)
2 Chr. 6:23	by **requiting** the wicked (by *repaying* the guilty)
2 Chr. 6:24	if thy people be **put to the worse before** the enemy (*defeated*)
2 Chr. 6:37	if they **bethink themselves** in the land (*have a change of heart*)
2 Chr. 8:13	even after a certain rate every day (*according to the daily requirements*)
2 Chr. 10:10	My little finger shall be thicker than my father's **loins** (than my father's *waist*).
2 Chr. 18:9	[the two kings] sat in a **void** (sat in an *open area*)
2 Chr. 25:16	Then the prophet **forbare** (the prophet *stopped*)
2 Chr. 25:22	Judah was **put to the worse** (Judah was *routed* by Israel)
2 Chr. 26:14	Uzziah prepared **habergeons** (provided *coats of armor*)

2 Chr. 26:15	he [invented] **engines** (*instruments to shoot arrows*)	
2 Chr. 26:18	it **appertaineth** not unto thee (*it is not right for you*)	
2 Chr. 34:4	he **strowed** [dust] upon the graves (he *scattered* dust)	
2 Chr. 34:11	they gave the **artificers** [money] (*carpenters and builders*)	
2 Chr. 36:3	the king of Egypt **condemned** the land (*imposed a levy*)	
2 Chr. 36:4	and **turned** his name (and *changed* his name)	
Ezra 3:12	**ancient men** (*older priests, Levites* and *family heads*)	
Ezra 4:13	thou shalt **endamage** the revenue (royal revenues will *suffer*)	
Ezra 4:14	we have **certified** the king (we are sending this message to *inform* the king)	
Ezra 4:17	**peace, and at such a time** (a *customary greeting*)	
Ezra 6:1	the **house of the rolls** (the *archives*)	
Ezra 8:36	the king's **lieutenants** (the royal *satraps* and *governors*)	
Ezra 9:3	I sat down **astoined** (I sat down *appalled*)	
Neh. 2:7	that they may **convey me over** (*provide me safe conduit*)	
Neh. 2:8	the gates of the palace which **appertained** (the gates of the citadel *by the temple*)	
Neh. 2:13	before the **dragon well** (the *jackal's drinking hole*)	
Neh. 2:13	to the **dung port** (the *manure gate*)	
Neh. 3:19	another **piece over against the going up** (*from a point facing the ascent*)	
Neh. 3:27	the great **tower that lieth out** (the great *projecting tower*)	

Neh. 4:17	**with those that laded** (those *who carried the materials*)	
Neh. 5:17	were **chargeable unto the people** (*placed a heavy burden on the people*)	
Neh. 8:9	Nehemiah who is the **Tirshatha** (a transliteration meaning: *the governor*)	
Neh. 9:32	the **terrible** God (the *awesome* God)	
Neh. 12:24	**ward over against ward** ([teams of praise] *one section responding to the other*)	
Esther 2:10	Esther had not **shewed her people** (not *revealed her nationality*)	
Esther 2:23	when **inquisition** was made (when the report was *investigated*)	
Esther 3:6	he **thought scorn** to lay hands on (he *scorned the idea* of)	
Esther 3:13	**take the spoil of them for a prey** (to *plunder their goods*)	
Esther 4:14	then shall **enlargement arise** (*deliverance will come*)	
Esther 7:4	the enemy could not **countervail** (*cannot be compared with* the loss the king would suffer)	
Job 1:8	one who **escheweth** evil (a man who *shuns* evil)	
Job 3:12	why did the knees **prevent** me? (Why were there knees to *receive me at birth? Why was I born?*)	
Job 4:2	if we **assay to commune** (if someone *ventures a word with you*)	
Job 9:33	any **daysman** betwixt us (*someone to arbitrate between us*)	
Job 15:26	the **thick bosses of his bucklers** (a *thick, strong shield*)	
Job 15:27	maketh **collops of fat on his flanks** (his *waist bulges with flesh*)	

Job 15:35	their **belly** prepareth deceit (their *womb* fashions deceit)
Job 16:15	**defile my horn in the dust** (*my strength* or *power* was defiled)
Job 17:6	**aforetime I was as a tabret** (*a man in whose face people spit*)
Job 18:9	the **gin** shall take him by the heel (a *trap* seizes him by the heel)
Job 20:3	I have heard the **check of my reproach** (the *rebuke that puts me to shame; dishonors me*)
Job 21:29	do ye not know their **tokens**? (pay no regard to their *accounts*)
Job 30:27	my **bowels boiled** (my *emotions churned* or *were in turmoil*)
Job 30:27	days of affliction **prevented** me (*days of suffering confront me*)
Job 30:31	my **organ** is turned into the voice of them that weep (my *flute* is turned to the sound of wailing)
Job 31:40	let **cockle** grow (let *weeds* come up instead of barley)
Job 32:6	I **durst** not (I *dared* not; *not daring* to tell you)
Job 36:26	Who hath **enjoined** God (*prescribed his ways for him?*)
Job 38:11	**hitherto** shalt thou come (*this far* you may come and no farther)
Job 39:4	their young ones are **in good liking** (their young *thrive*)
Job 39:4	they grow up **with corn** (they grow strong *in the wilds*)
Job 40:15	[I, God, made] **behemoth** (*hippopotamus* or *elephant*)
Job 41:18	by his **neesing** a light doth shine (his *snoring* throws out flashes of light)
Job 41:25	by reason of **breakings** they **purify themselves** (*terrified* by the *crashing noises*)

Hab. 2:7

(plunder)

Psalm 4:2	seek after **leasing** (seek after *falsehood*; seek *false gods*)
Psalm 18:5	the snares of death **prevented** me (were *round about me*; the cords of the grave *coiled around me*)
Psalm 18:26	with the **froward** thou wilt show thyself **froward** (to the *crooked* you show yourself *shrewd*)
Psalm 22:20	deliver my **darling** from the power of the dog (deliver my *precious life* from the power of the dogs)
Psalm 22:21	**unicorns** (*wild oxen*)
Psalm 34:10	they who seek the Lord shall **not want** any good thing (*lack* no good thing)
Psalm 35:15	the **abjects** were against me (*attackers* gathered against me)
Psalm 37:14	such as are **upright conversation** (those whose *ways are upright*)
Psalm 45:1	my heart is **inditing** a good matter (*stirred* by noble theme)
Psalm 45:4	thy right hand shalt teach thee **terrible** things (let your right hand display *awesome* deeds)
Psalm 55:19	because they **have no changes** (because they *never experience spiritual growth*)
Psalm 59:15	and **grudge** if they are not satisfied (*howl* if they are not satisfied)
Psalm 68:13	ye have **lien among the pots** (while *you sleep among the campfires*)
Psalm 73:4	no **bands** in their death (no *struggles* in their death)
Psalm 74:4	set up their **ensigns** for signs (set up their *banners* as signs)

Psalm 75:8	the wicked shall **wring them out** (*drink it down to its very dregs*)
Psalm 77:8	Is His mercy **clean gone**? (Has His mercy *failed for all time*?)
Psalm 78:30	they were not **estranged from their lust** (*before they turned from the food they craved*)
Psalm 78:31	God slew the **fattest** of them (put to death the *strongest* among them)
Psalm 78:45	He sent **divers** flies among them. (He sent *swarms of flies* that devoured them.)
Psalm 88:13	In the morning my prayer **prevent** thee. (In the morning my prayer *comes before* you.)
Psalm 94:8	ye **brutish** among the people (*senseless ones* among the people)
Psalm 106:29	provoked him to anger with their **inventions** (their *wicked deeds*)
Psalm 107:39	they are **minished** and brought low (their *numbers decreased* and *they were humbled*)
Psalm 137:7	**Rase it, rase it** (Tear it down; tear it down.)
Psalm 139:2	Thou knowest my **uprisings**. (You know *when I rise*.)
Psalm 139:15	I was **curiously wrought** (I was *made in the secret place*)
Psalm 139:16	yet being **unperfect** (Your eyes saw my *unformed* body.)
Prov. 1:4	to give **subtilty** to the simple (giving *prudence* to the simple)
Prov. 2:12	men that speak **froward things** (*whose words are perverse*)
Prov. 6:1	if thou hast **stricken thy hand** (*struck hands in pledge*)

Prov. 6:3	**make sure thy friend** (*press your plea with your neighbor*)
Prov. 6:12	a **naughty person** (a *scoundrel* and a *villain*)
Prov. 8:12	find out knowledge of **witty inventions** (*possess knowledge* and *carry out clever plans*)
Prov. 9:4	him that **wanteth** understanding (all who are *simple*)
Prov. 9:15	call **passengers** who go right (calling out to *those who pass by*)
Prov. 12:1	he that hateth reproof is **brutish** (who hates correction is *stupid*)
Prov. 12:24	the slothful shall be **under tribute** (laziness ends in *slave labor*)
Prov. 15:27	He that hateth **gifts** shall live. (He who hates *bribes* will live.)
Prov. 17:9	he that **coverth** a transgression (he who *covers over an offense*)
Prov. 20:10	**divers** weights are an abomination (*Differing weights and differing measures* the Lord detests them both.)
Prov. 23:20	be not among **riotous eaters of flesh** (the *gluttonous*, those who *gorge themselves on meat*)
Prov. 23:31	Look not upon wine when it **moveth itself aright**. (when it *goes down smoothly*)
Prov. 25:4	there shall come forth a vessel for the **finer** (*refiner*, out comes material for the *silversmith*)
Prov. 25:20	as vinegar upon **nitre** (like vinegar poured on *soda*)
Prov. 27:22	**bray** a fool in a mortar with a pestle (*crush a fool into powder*)
Prov. 28:22	he that **hasteth** to be rich (he who is *eager* to get rich)
Prov. 29:24	he **bewrayeth** it not (he is *put under oath* and dares not testify)

Prov. 30:26	The **conies are but a feeble folk** (The *rock badgers are creatures of little power*.)
S of S 1:14	as a cluster of **camphire** (as a cluster of *henna blossoms*)
S of S 2:5	**Stay me with flagons.** (*Strengthen me with cakes of raisins.*)
S of S 2:12	the voice of the **turtle** is heard (*turtledove*)
S of S 5:5	My hands **dropped** with myrrh (My hands *dripped* with myrrh.)
S of S 7:5	The king is **held in the galleries.** (*held captive by its tresses*)
S of S 7:8	the **smell of thy nose** (an idiom meaning: the *fragrance of your breath*)
Isaiah 1:13	I cannot **away with** (I cannot *bear* your evil assemblies.)
Isaiah 1:24	I will **ease me** of mine adversaries. (I will *get rid of* my foes.)
Isaiah 1:31	The strong shall be as **tow**. (The mighty men will become *tinder*.)
Isaiah 2:6	because they be **replenished** (They are *full of superstition; they practice divination.*)
Isaiah 3:16	with **wanton eyes** (*flirting with their eyes*)
Isaiah 3:16	making a **tinkling with their feet** (with *ankle ornaments jingling on their ankles*)
Isaiah 3:17	The Lord will **discover their secret parts** (*make their scalps bald*)
Isaiah 3:18	The Lord will take away their **cauls** and their **round tires like the moon**. (their *headbands*; their *crescent necklaces*)
Isaiah 3:22	the **changeable suits of apparel** (the *fine robes*)
Isaiah 3:22	the **wimples**, the **crisping pins** (the *cloaks, handbags, purses*)

Isaiah 3:24	instead of **stomacher** (instead of a *robe*)
Isaiah 5:12	the **viol**, the **tabret**, and **pipe** (*lyres, tambourines,* and *flutes*)
Isaiah 8:21	shall pass through it **hardly bestead** (*distressed and hungry*)
Isaiah 9:1	the **dimness shall not be such as was in her vexation** (There will be *no gloom for those who were in distress*.)
Isaiah 9:3	Thou hast **not increased** the joy (a mistranslation: Literally, You have *increased* their joy.)
Isaiah 10:23	The Lord shall **make a consumption**. (The Lord Almighty will *carry out the destruction*.)
Isaiah 10:28	He hath **laid up his carriages** (*stored supplies*)
Isaiah 13:21	And **satyrs** shall dance there. (*Wild goats* will leap about.)
Isaiah 14:23	a **bittern** (a *place for owls*)
Isaiah 18:7	a people scattered and **peeled** (*tall and smooth-skinned*)
Isaiah 19:9	they that weave **networks** (weavers of *fine linen*)
Isaiah 21:14	They **prevented with their bread him that fled**. (They *brought food for the fugitives*.)
Isaiah 22:2	thou that art full of **stirs** (full of *commotion*)
Isaiah 22:16	that **graveth** an habitation for himself (to *carve out a grave*)
Isaiah 23:3	she is a **mart** of nations (the *marketplace* for the nations)
Isaiah 24:2	as with the taker of **usury**, so with the giver of **usury** (*interest; for debtor as for creditor*)
Isaiah 28:4	like the **hasty** fruit (like a *fig ripe before harvest*)

Isaiah 28:25	cast abroad the **fitches** (*dill*; Does he not *sow caraway*?)
Isaiah 28:28	the **bread is bruised** (*grain must be ground to make bread*)
Isaiah 29:7	fight against her **munition** (*stronghold, attack her fortress*)
Isaiah 30:6	the **bunches** of camels (on the *humps* of camels)
Isaiah 30:12	and **stay** on them (*relied on oppression*)
Isaiah 30:24	that **ear** the ground (that *till* the ground)
Isaiah 31:9	young men shall be **discomfited** (*put to forced labor*)
Isaiah 32:8	The **liberal** deviseth **liberal** things. (The noble man makes noble things.)
Isaiah 32:12	They shall **lament for the teats**. (They shall *beat their breasts*.)
Isaiah 34:11	the **cormorant** and the **bittern** (*desert owl* and *screech owl*)
Isaiah 34:16	None of them shall **want** her mate. (Not one will *lack* her mate.)
Isaiah 43:17	quenched as **tow** (snuffed out like a *wick*)
Isaiah 43:24	**made me to serve** with thy sins (*burdened me* with your sins)
Isaiah 46:4	even to **hoar** hairs (even to your *gray hair*)
Isaiah 46:12	Hearken unto me, ye **stout-hearted.** (you *stubborn-hearted*)
Isaiah 47:8	thou that dwellest **carelessly** (who live *securely*; *lounging in your security*)
Isaiah 57:17	he went on **frowardly** (*backsliding*, kept on in his *willful ways*)
Isaiah 63:15	the **sounding of thy bowels** (the *stirring of your compassion*)
Isaiah 64:9	Be not **wroth very sore** (*angry beyond measure*)
Jer. 2:27	saying to the **stock**, Thou art my father (saying to a *tree*)

Jer. 2:33	**Why trimmest thou thy way to seek love?** (*How skilled you are at pursuing love!*)
Jer. 2:26	**Why gladdest thou about?** (*Why do you go about so much?*)
Jer. 4:22	They are **sottish** children. (They are *senseless* children.)
Jer. 4:30	thou **rentest thy face with painting** (*shade your eyes with paint*)
Jer. 5:30	A **wonderful thing is committed**. (*horrible thing has happened*)
Jer. 10:22	the **noise of the bruit** is come (*sound of a rumor; report*)
Jer. 14:4	the ground is **chapt** (the ground is *cracked*)
Jer. 17:10	I **try the reins** (I *test the conscience; examine the mind*)
Jer. 19:4	they have **estranged** this place (they have *desecrated* this place)
Jer. 19:9	**straitness** with which their enemies shall **straiten** them (*distress*; the *stress of the siege imposed on* them by their enemies)
Jer. 20:9	I could not **stay** (I could not *refrain*)
Jer. 20:10	all my **familiars watched** (all my *friends are waiting*)
Jer. 22:14	it is **ceiled** with cedar (it is *paneled* with cedar)
Jer. 24:2	One basket had very good figs and the other basket had very **naughty** figs. (*bad, spoiled figs*)
Jer. 25:24	the kings of the **mingled people** (the kings of the *foreign people*)
Jer. 27:7	great kings **serve themselves of him** (*enslave, subjugate*)
Jer. 31:18	**turn me and I shall be turned** (*restore* me and I will *return*)
Jer. 32:10	I **subscribed the evidence** (I *signed and sealed the deed*)
Jer. 36:16	they were afraid both **oneandother** (*looked at each other in fear*)

[Mary] "...<u>saluted</u> Elizabeth."

Luke 1:40

(greeted, *or* hugged)

Jer. 46:4	put on the **brigandines** (*coats of mail*; put on your *armor*)
Jer. 48:6	like the **heath** in the wilderness (*shrub*, like a *bush* in the desert)
Jer. 48:19	stand by the way and **espy** (stand by the road and *watch*)
Jer. 50:36	they shall **dote** (they will *become fools*)
Jer. 51:2	I will send unto Babylon **fanners** (*winnowers*)
Jer. 51:17	every **founder** is confounded (every *goldsmith* is shamed)
Jer. 51:19	he is the **former** of all things (He is the *Maker* of all things)
Lam. 4:10	women have **sodden** their own children (women have *cooked* their own children)
Ezek. 1:18	their **rings** were full of eyes (the *edges* or *rims of the wheels*)
Ezek. 6:9	because of their **whorish** heart (by their *adulterous* hearts)
Ezek. 7:7	not the **sounding again** of the mountains (not *joyful shouting* upon the mountains)
Ezek. 12:3	prepare thee **stuff for removing** (pack your *belongings* for exile)
Ezek. 13:18	Woe to the women that sew **pillows to all arm-holes** (who sew *magic charms to the sleeves' ends*)
Ezek. 14:15	if I cause **noisome** beasts to pass through (*evil* or *wild beasts*)
Ezek. 16:4	thou wast not **swaddled** at all (you were not *wrapped in cloths*)
Ezek. 16:34	**the contrary is in thee** (*you are the opposite of others*)
Ezek. 21:10	it is **furbished that it may glitter** (*polished to flash like lightening*)

Ezek. 21:14	great men which entereth into their **privy** chambers (*private*)
Ezek. 21:19	both **twain** shall come forth out of one land (*both of them*)
Ezek. 23:10	she became **famous** among women (she became a *byword*)
Ezek. 24:23	and your **tires** shall be upon your heads (your *fancy headdress* or *turbans* will be on your heads)
Ezek. 28:18	the iniquity of thy **traffick** (your *dishonest trade*)
Ezek. 29:7	madest all their **loins to be at a stand** (*inward parts to shake*)
Ezek. 30:21	to put a **roller** to bind it (put in a *splint* and bind it)
Ezek. 35:6	**sith** thou has not hated blood (*since* you did not hate bloodshed)
Ezek. 37:11	we are cut off **for our parts** (we were cut off *on our part*)
Ezek. 39:14	they shall **sever out men of continual employment** (*men will be chosen to be regularly employed*)
Ezek. 43:14	from the **lesser settle** to the **greater settle** (from the *smaller ledge* up to the *larger ledge*)
Ezek. 44:20	**poll** their heads (*keep the hair of their heads trimmed*)
Ezek. 45:10	Ye shall have a **just bath** (*accurate liquid measure*: Bath = 7½ gallons)
Ezek. 45:11	the measure thereof shall be after the **homer** (according to a measure of *eight bushels*)
Ezek. 46:14	to **temper** the fine flour (to *moisten* the fine flour)
Ezek. 47:11	**marishers** shall **not be healed** (*marshes* will *not become fresh*)
Daniel 1:12	let them give **pulse** to eat (give us nothing but *vegetables*)

Daniel 3:5	the sound of the **sackbut** and **dulcimer** (*zither* and *pipes*)
Daniel 3:16	we are **not careful to answer thee** (*we do not need to defend ourselves before you in this matter*)
Daniel 3:21	these men were bound in their **hosen** (bound in their *trousers*)
Daniel 5:6	the **joints of his loins were loosed** (*his legs gave way*)
Daniel 5:6	his **knees smote one against another** (knees *knocked together*)
Daniel 11:34	they shall be **holpen** with a little help (will receive a little help)
Hosea 9:1	a reward upon every **cornfloor** (at every *threshing floor*)
Hosea 14:2	**render the calves** of our lips (*give forth the praise* of our lips; *offer the fruit* of our lips)
Joel 1:7	he hath made it **clean bare** (he *stripped off the bark*)
Joel 1:7	he hath **barked** my fig trees (*ruined* my fig trees)
Joel 1:13	**howl**, ye ministers (*wail*, you temple workers)
Amos 4:5	for this **liketh** you (for this is what *you love to do*)
Amos 5:21	I will not **smell** in your solemn assemblies (I do not *enjoy the fragrance of* or *take delight* in your solemn assemblies)
Obadiah 1:7	they have **laid a wound** under thee (they have *set a trap* for you)
Jonah 1:11	for the sea **wrought** (the sea *raged*)
Micah 1:4	the mountains shall **be molten** (the mountains shall *melt*)

Acts 5:6

(wrapped)

Micah 7:3	so they **wrap it up** (literally: they *weave it together*; an idiom meaning: *they all conspire together*)
Nahum 1:10	they are **folden together** (they will be *entangled among thorns*)
Nahum 2:5	he shall **recount his worthies** (he *summons his picked troops*)
Nahum 2:7	her maids shall lead her **tabering** upon their breasts (*beating upon their breasts*)
Nahum 2:12	filled his dens with **ravin** (filling his dens with *the prey*)
Nahum 3:19	all that hear the **bruit** of thee (the *news* about you)
Hab. 1:9	their **faces shall sup up as the east wind** (an idiom meaning: their *hordes advance like a desert wind*)
Hab. 2:7	thou shalt be for **booties** unto them (their *plunder*)
Hab. 2:13	people shall **labor in the very fire** (*people's labor is only fuel for the fire*)
Hab. 3:13	by **discovering the foundation unto the neck** (by *stripping him head to foot*)
Zeph. 2:9	the **breeding of nettles** (a *place of weeds*)
Zeph. 3:19	I will save her that **halteth** (I will *rescue the lame*)
Haggai 2:16	when one came to the **pressfat** (when anyone went to a *wine vat*)
Zech. 1:21	these are come to **fray** them (to *terrify* them)
Zech. 3:5	let them set a **fair mitre** upon his head (a *clean turban*)
Zech. 6:6	the **grisled** go forth (the *dappled horses* go forth)
Malachi 1:13	ye have **snuffed at it** (*sniffed at it contemptuously*)

Matthew 3:4	a **leathern girdle** about his **loins** (a *leather belt around his waist*)
Matthew 3:12	He will **throughly purge** his floor (*clear his threshing floor*)
Matthew 3:12	gather his wheat into his **garner** (into his *barn*)
Matthew 3:15	then he **suffered** him (then John *consented*)
Matthew 5:33	thou shalt not **forswear** thyself (do not *break your oath*)
Matthew 6:6	when thou prayest, enter into thy **closet** (your *private room*)
Matthew 9:30	Jesus **straitly charged** them (Jesus *warned them sternly*)
Matthew 10:10	provide not a **scrip** for your journey (take no *bag of money*)
Matthew 10:10	nor yet **staves** (nor a *staff*)
Matthew 13:21	but **dureth** for a while (but *lasts* only a short time)
Matthew 13:25	sowed **tares** among the wheat (sowed *weeds* among the wheat)
Matthew 14:11	his head was brought on a **charger** (on a *platter*)
Matthew 15:26	it is not **meet** to take the children's bread (it is not *right*)
Matthew 16:3	the sky is red and **lowring** (the sky is red and *overcast*)
Matthew 19:14	Jesus said, **Suffer** little children to come unto me (*permit*)
Matthew 21:2	go into the village **over against** you (*ahead of you*)
Matthew 21:3	and if any man say **ought** unto you (says *anything* to you)
Matthew 21:31	.Which of them **twain**? (Which of *the two*?)
Matthew 21:33	. **let it out to husbandmen** (*rented* the vineyard to some *farmers*)
Matthew 22:6	and **intreated** them **spitefully** (and *treated them shamefully*)
Matthew 24:7	earthquakes in **divers** places (in *different* places, *various* places)

Matthew 26:65	then the high pries **rent** his clothes (*tore* his clothes)
Matthew 26:69	a **damsel** came unto him (a *servant girl* came to him)
Matthew 26:73	thy speech **bewrayeth** thee (your *accent gives you away*)
Matthew 27:15	the governor was **wont** to release (it was the governor's *custom*)
Matthew 27:50	**yielded up the ghost** (*died*, gave up his spirit)
Matthew 27:51	the veil of the temple was **rent in twain** (*torn in two*)
Mark 1:30	**anon** they tell him of her (*right away* they told Jesus about her)
Mark 1:43	and he **straitly charged** him (*sternly warned*)
Mark 1:45	to **blaze abroad** the matter (to *spread the news*)
Mark 2:1	and it was **noised** that he was in the house (it was *reported*; *the people heard* that he had come home)
Mark 2:4	they could not **come nigh** unto him for the **press** (they could not *get him to Jesus* because of the *crowd*)
Mark 2:15	as Jesus **sat at meat** (while Jesus was *having dinner*)
Mark 5:37	**save** Peter, James and John (*except for* Peter, James and John)
Mark 6:33	and ran **afoot thither** out of all cities, and **outwent** them (and ran *on foot from all the towns* and *got there ahead of them*)
Mark 9:6	for he **wist not** what to say; for they were **sore afraid** (he *did not know* what to say, they were so *frightened*)
Mark 9:12	he must suffer many things and be **set at nought** (*treated with contempt*; he must suffer much and be *rejected*)
Mark 9:13	they have done to him whatsoever they **listed** (*wished*)

Mark 9:19	How long shall I **suffer** you? (How long shall I *put up with* you?)
Mark 9:26	the spirit cried out and **rent him sore** (*convulsed him violently*)
Mark 10:1	and as **he was wont** (as *was his custom*)
Mark 10:8	so they are no more **twain**, but one flesh (no more *two*, but one)
Mark 11:13	if **haply** he might find anything on it (if *perhaps*)
Mark 14:44	he had given them a **token** (arranged a *signal* with them)
Luke 1:29	she **cast in her mind** what manner of **salutation** (she *wondered* what kind of *greeting* this might be)
Luke 1:40	and Mary **saluted** Elizabeth (*greeted* or *hugged* Elizabeth)
Luke 9:29	the **fashion of his countenance** (the *appearance of his face*)
Luke 9:41	thou art **careful** about many things (*worried* and *upset*)
Luke 11:8	because of his **importunity** (the man's *persistence* and *boldness*)
Luke 11:27	blessed are the **paps which thou hast sucked** (blessed is the *mother who gave you birth and nursed you*)
Luke 11:39	but your inward part is full of **ravening** (you are full of *greed* and *wickedness*)
Luke 11:42	ye tithe **mint and rue** (an idiom meaning: you *give God a tenth of all you grow*)
Luke 12:33	how I am **straitened** till it be accomplished (how *distressed* I am until it is completed)
Luke 12:58	lest he **hale** thee to the judge (he may *drag you off* to the judge)
Luke 14:8	sit not in the **highest room** (do not take the *place of honor*)

Luke 14:32	he sendeth an **ambassage** (he will send a *delegation*)
Luke 16:9	make to yourselves friends **of the mammon** (use *worldly wealth* to gain friends for yourselves)
Luke 17:9	I **trow** not (I *think* not)
Luke 18:32	spitefully **entreated** (they will *mock him, insult him*)
Luke 21:4	she of her **penury hath cast in all** (she out of her *poverty* put in *all she had to live on*)
Luke 23:32	two other **malefactors** were led with him (two other *criminals*)
John 2:47	in whom is **no guile** (*no hypocrisy, nothing false*)
John 5:3	of **impotent** folk, **halt, withered** (*disabled people* who were *lame* or *paralyzed*)
John 5:13	Jesus had **conveyed** himself away (Jesus had *slipped away*)
John 5:21	the Son **quickeneth** whom he will (the Son *gives life* to whom he is pleased to give it)
John 13:26	I shall give a **sop** (a *piece of bread dipped in gravy*)
Acts 2:6	when this was **noised abroad** (when they *heard this*)
Acts 3:24	that he should **be holden of it** (it was *impossible for death to keep its hold on him*)
Acts 5:2	**being privy** of it (with his wife's *full knowledge* of it)
Acts 5:6	the young men arose, **wound him up** (*wrapped up his body*)
Acts 5:10	then fell she down **straitway** at his feet (*immediately*)
Acts 5:10	and she **yielded up the ghost** (and *she died*)

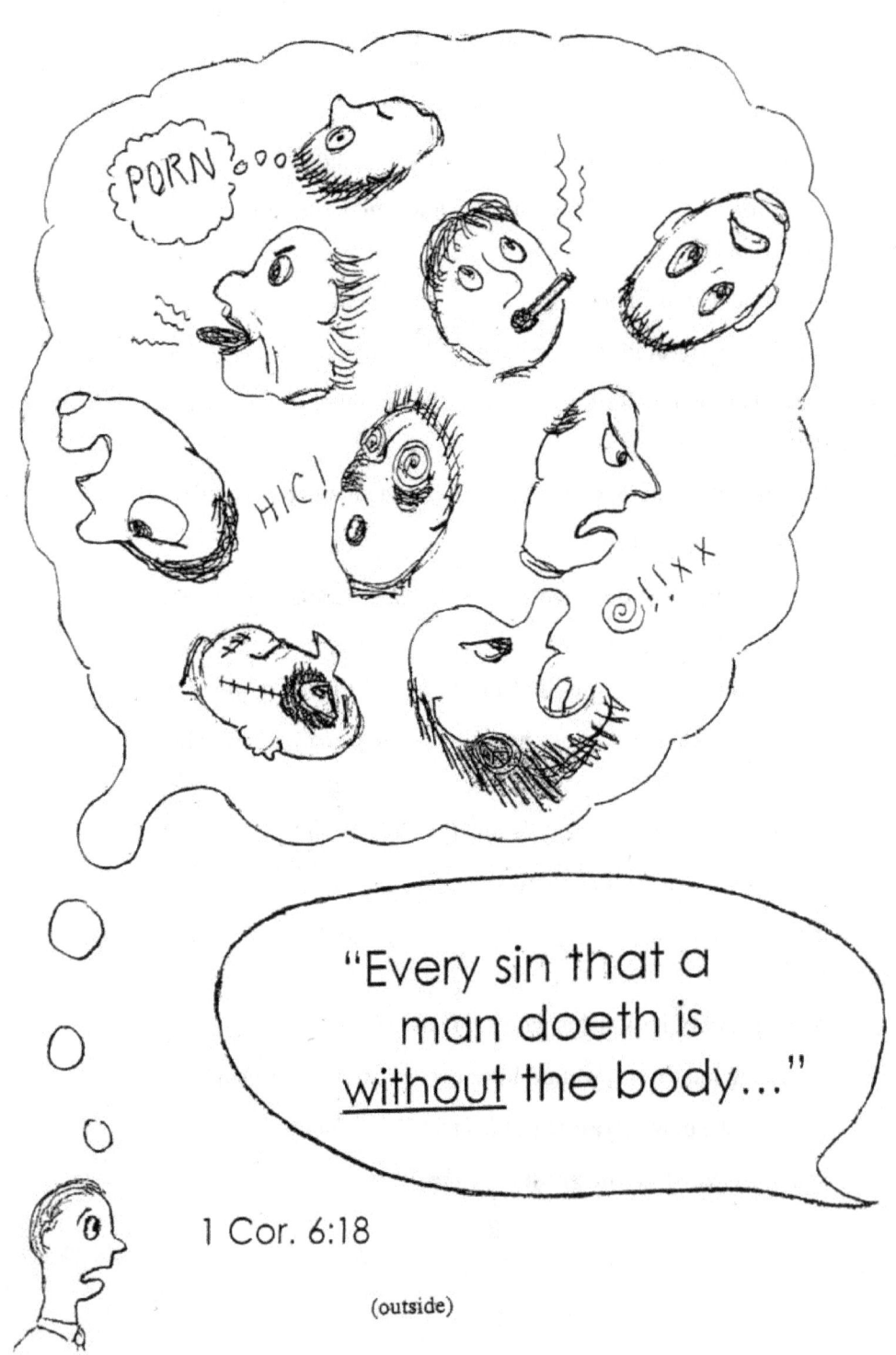

Acts 7:19	and **evil entreated** our fathers (he *oppressed* our forefathers)
Acts 9:5	kick against the pricks (kick against the goads)
Acts 9:24	their **laying await** (they *kept close watch* on the city gates)
Acts 9:26	Saul **assayed** to join himself (Saul *tried* to join the disciples)
Acts 10:29	I came without **gainsaying** (without *raising any objections*)
Acts 13:36	David **fell on sleep** (David *fell asleep, died*)
Acts 17:4	some of them **consorted with** Paul (some of them *joined* Paul)
Acts 17:34	certain men **clave unto** him (*became followers* of Paul)
Acts 18:7	whose house **joined hard to** (whose house *was next to*)
Acts 19:19	who used **curious arts** (*magical arts*; who had *practiced sorcery*)
Acts 19:38	let them **implead** one another (let them *accuse* one another)
Acts 19:40	give an account of this **concourse** (this *unruly gathering*)
Acts 20:26	I **take you to record** (I *declare to you* today)
Acts 20:37	they **fell upon Paul's neck** (they *embraced* him)
Acts 20:37	they all wept **sore** (they all wept *bitterly*)
Acts 21:1	after we were **gotten** from there (after we had *torn ourselves away* from them)
Acts 24:22	to **know the uttermost of your matter** (I will *decide your case*)
Acts 26:5	after the most **straitest sect** (the *strictest sect* of our religion)
Acts 27:16	**running under** a certain island (*sailing past*, on the *calm side*)
Acts 27:17	they **strake sale** (they *lowered the sea anchors*)

Acts 27:30	they acted **under color** (*pretending*)
Acts 28:2	the **barbarous** people showed us **no little kindness** (the *islanders* showed us *unusual kindness*)
Acts 28:4	**vengeance suffereth not** to live (*Justice has not allowed* to live)
Romans 1:13	was **let hitherto** (has been *prevented from doing so until now*)
Romans 4:17	who **quickeneth** the dead (who *gives life* to the dead)
Romans 7:8	**wrought in me all manner of concupiscence** (*produced in me every kind of covetous desire*)
Romans 10:21	unto a **gainsaying** people (to an *obstinate* people)
Romans 11:14	provoke to **emulation** (*provoke to jealousy, arouse to envy*)
Romans 12:9	Let love be without **dissimulation** (without *hypocrisy, sincere*)
Romans 12:12	continuing **instant** in prayer (*diligently, faithful* in prayer)
Romans 13:13	walk not in **chambering** and **wantonness** (don't walk in *sexual immorality* and *debauchery*)
Romans 14:4	he shall be **holden up** (he will *stand*)
1 Cor. 3:9	ye are God's **husbandry** (you are God's *cultivated field*)
1 Cor. 6:18	every sin that a man doeth is **without** the body (all others sins a man commits are *outside his body*)
1 Cor. 7:5	that Satan tempt you not for your **incontinency** (for your *lack of sexual restraint*)
1 Cor. 10:25	whatsoever is sold in the **shambles** (the *meat market*)
1 Cor. 13:4	charity **vaunteth** not itself (love *does not boast*)

1 Cor. 16:13	**quit you like men** (*be men of courage*)
1 Cor. 16:15	they have **addicted** themselves (*appointed* or *devoted*)
1 Cor. 16:22	let him be **Anathema Maranatha** (a transliteration meaning: let him be *accursed*; *our Lord is coming*)
2 Cor. 2:5	that I may not **overcharge** you all (be *severe* or *overbearing*)
2 Cor. 2:7	**so that contrariwise** ye ought to forgive (*otherwise, instead*)
2 Cor. 6:2	I have **succoured** thee (I *helped* you)
2 Cor. 8:1	**we do you to wit of** (*we want you to know*)
2 Cor. 9:1	it is **superfluous** for me to write you (there is *no need* for me)
2 Cor. 9:2	the **forwardness** of your mind (the *readiness* of your mind; your *eagerness*)
2 Cor. 9:13	by the **experiment of this ministration** (because of the *service by which you have proved yourselves*)
2 Cor. 10:6	to **revenge** all disobedience (to *punish* every act of disobedience)
2 Cor. 11:5	I was not **a whit behind** (I am not *in the least inferior* to)
2 Cor. 11:29	Who is offended and I **burn** not? (and I am *not ashamed*)
2 Cor. 12:20	lest there be **swellings** (lest there be *conceit, arrogance*)
2 Cor. 12:21	**lasciviousness which they have committed** (*debauchery in which they have indulged*)
2 Cor. 13:6	we are not **reprobates** (we are not *discredited*; we have not *failed the test*)

Galatians 3:5	no man **disannulleth** [a legal document] (no man *annuls it;* no one can *set it aside*)
Galatians 4:18	it is good to be **zealously affected** (it is *fine to be zealous*)
Galatians 4:24	which **gendereth** bondage (*bearing children to be slaves*)
Galatians 5:12	I would they were even **cut off** (*emasculate themselves*)
Galatians 5:19	works of the flesh are **variance, emulations** (*discord, jealousy*)
Phil. 1:14	**waxing** confident (*becoming confident, encouraged*)
Phil. 1:23	I am in a **strait betwixt two** (*torn between the two decisions*)
Phil. 2:1	if any **bowels and mercies** (*tenderness* and *compassion*)
Phil. 3:12	that I may **apprehend** that for which also I am **apprehended** (*I press on to take hold of that for which He took hold of me*)
Phil. 4:6	**be careful for nothing** (*don't worry about anything*)
Col. 2:8	**beware lest any man spoil you** (*see to it that no one takes you captive*)
Col. 2:15	and having **spoiled** principalities and powers (having *disarmed* the powers and authorities)
Col. 2:18	let no man **beguile** you (don't let anyone *disqualify* you)
Col. 2:20	the **rudiments** of the world (the *basic principles* of this world)
Col. 3:5	evil **concupiscence** (evil *desires*)
Col. 3:25	there is **no respect of persons** (there is *no favoritism*)
1 Thes. 4:15	we shall not **prevent** them who are asleep (we will not *precede* those who have fallen asleep)

1 Thes. 5:14	**comfort the feebleminded** (*encourage the timid*)
2 Thes. 2:7	he who **letteth will let** (he who *hinders will continue to hinder*)
1 Tim. 1:9-10	the law is for **men-stealers** (the law if for *kidnapers, slave traders*)
1 Tim. 3:13	purchase to themselves a **good degree** (to *gain an excellent standing*)
1 Tim. 5:1	**intreat** him as a father (*exhort* him as if he were your father)
1 Tim. 5:11	begun to **wax wanton** (begin to *grow in sensual desires*)
1 Tim. 5:22	lay hands **suddenly** on no man (*do not be hasty* in the laying on of hands—that is, to appoint someone to a position of responsibility)
2 Tim. 2:17	their word will eat as doth a **canker** (their teaching will spread like *gangrene*)
2 Tim. 2:25	if God **peradventure** will give them repentance (if God by *any means, in the hope that God will grant repentance*)
2 Tim. 4:2	be **instant** in season (be *prepared* in season and out of season)
Titus 1:12	the Cretans are **slow bellies** (the Cretans are *lazy gluttons*)
Philemon 18	or oweth the **ought** (or owes you *anything*)
Philemon 20	**refresh my bowels** (*gladden my heart*)
Hebrews 7:26	for such an high priest **became** us (*meets our need*)

Hebrews 11:29	the Egyptians, **assaying** to do, were drowned (when the Egyptians *tried to do so*)
Hebrews 12:1	which doth so easily **beset** us (that so easily *entangle* us)
Hebrews 13:6	to do good and to **communicate** forget not (to *share with others*)
James 1:5	and **upbraideth** not (*without finding fault*)
James 1:21	**lay apart all superfluity of naughtiness** (*put away all overflowing of wickedness; get rid of all moral filth and the evil that is so prevalent*)
James 2:3	weareth the **gay** clothing (*wearing fine clothes*)
Jams 3:4	wherever the **governor listeth** (wherever the *pilot wants to go*)
James 5:11	and have seen **the end of the Lord** (and have seen *what the Lord finally brought about*)
1 Peter 1:13	**gird up the loins** of your mind (*prepare your minds for action*)
1 Peter 1:22	**unfeigned love** of the brethren (*sincere love*)
1 Peter 3:3	**plaiting** the hair (*braiding* the hair)
1 Peter 3:9	not rendering **railing for railing** (*do not repay insult for insult*)
2 Peter 2:13	**sporting** themselves with their own **deceiving** (*reveling in their pleasures*)
2 Peter 2:18	those that **were clean escaped** (who *are just escaping*)
2 Peter 3:16	they that are unlearned and unstable **wrest** (which ignorant and unstable *distort*)

1 Tim. 5:22

(Do not be hasty in the laying on of hands.)

1 John 2:2	He is the **propitiation** for our sins (the *atoning sacrifice*)
3 John 10	**prating against** us (*gossiping maliciously* about us)
Jude 1:6	they kept not their first **estate** (their first *positions of authority*)
Jude 1:9	**durst not** bring against him a **railing** accusation (did *not dare to bring a slanderous accusation*)
Jude 1:11	who perished in the **gainsaying** of Korah (in Korah's *rebellion*)
Rev. 2:23	he who searcheth the **reins** (he who searches *hearts* and *minds*)
Rev. 10:6	there should be **time no longer** (there will be *no more delay*)
Rev. 16:2	a **noisome** and **grievous** sore (*ugly* and *painful* sores)
Rev. 18:9	and lived **deliciously** with her (lived in *luxury* or *extravagantly* with her)
Rev. 18:22	the voice of **pipers** (the music of *flute players*)

www.ingramcontent.com/pod-product-compliance
Lightning Source LLC
Chambersburg PA
CBHW081323040426
42453CB00013B/2283